Spain

Jacques Casanova de Seingalt

[ZHINGOORA BOOKS]

This digital edition is published by
Zhingoora Books.

The Cover is Designed by Pallav Sethiya.

zhingoora_books@yahoo.com

SPAIN

CHAPTER I

I Am Ordered to Leave Vienna—The Empress Moderates but Does Not Annul the Order—Zavoiski at Munich—My Stay at Augsburg—Gasconnade at Louisburg—The Cologne Newspaper—My Arrival at Aix-la-Chapelle

The greatest mistake a man that punishes a knave can commit is to leave the said rogue alive, for he is certain to take vengeance. If I had had my sword in the den of thieves, I should no doubt have defended myself, but it would have gone ill with me, three against one, and I should probably have been cut to pieces, while the murderers would have escaped unpunished.

At eight o'clock Campioni came to see me in my bed, and was astonished at my adventure. Without troubling himself to compassionate me, we both began to think how we could get back my purse; but we came to the conclusion that it would be impossible, as I had nothing more than my mere assertion to prove the case. In spite of that, however, I wrote out the whole story, beginning with the girl who recited the Latin verses. I intended to bring the document before the police; however, I had not time to do so.

I was just sitting down to dinner, when an agent of the police came and gave me an order to go and speak to Count Schrotembach, the Statthalter. I told him to instruct my coachman, who was waiting at the door, and that I would follow him shortly.

When I called on the Statthalter, I found him to be a thick-set individual; he was standing up, and surrounded by men who seemed ready to execute his orders. When he saw me, he shewed me a watch, and requested me to note the hour.

"I see it."

"If you are at Vienna at that time to-morrow I shall have you expelled from the city."

"Why do you give me such an unjust order?"

"In the first place, I am not here to give you accounts or reasons for my actions. However, I may tell you that you are expelled for playing at games of chance, which are forbidden by the laws under pain of the galleys. Do you recognize that purse and these cards?"

I did not know the cards, but I knew the purse which had been stolen from me. I was in a terrible rage, and I only replied by presenting the magistrate with the truthful narrative of what had happened to me. He read it, and then said with a laugh that I was well known to be a man of parts, that my character was known, that I had been expelled from Warsaw, and that as for the document before him he judged it to be a pack of lies, since in his opinion it was altogether void of probability.

"In fine," he added, "you will obey my order to leave the town, and you must tell me where you are going."

"I will tell you that when I have made up my mind to go."

4

"What? You dare to tell me that you will not obey?"

"You yourself have said that if I do not go I shall be removed by force."

"Very good. I have heard you have a strong will, but here it will be of no use to you. I advise you to go quietly, and so avoid harsh measures."

"I request you to return me that document."

"I will not do so. Begone!"

This was one of the most terrible moments of my life. I shudder still when I think of it. It was only a cowardly love of life that hindered me from running my sword through the body of the Statthalter, who had treated me as if he were a hangman and not a judge.

As I went away I took it into my head to complain to Prince Kaunitz, though I had not the honour of knowing him. I called at his house, and a man I met told me to stay in the ante-chamber, as the prince would pass through to go to dinner.

It was five o'clock. The prince appeared, followed by his guests, amongst whom was M. Polo Renieri, the Venetian ambassador. The prince asked me what he could do for me, and I told my story in a loud voice before them all.

"I have received my order to go, but I shall not obey. I implore your highness to give me your protection, and to help me to bring my plea to the foot of the throne."

"Write out your petition," he replied, "and I will see that the empress gets it. But I advise you to ask her majesty for a respite, for if you say that you won't obey, she will be predisposed against you."

"But if the royal grace does not place me in security, I shall be driven away by violence."

"Then take refuge with the ambassador of your native country."

"Alas, my lord, my country has forsaken me. An act of legal though unconstitutional violence has deprived me of my rights as a citizen. My name is Casanova, and my country is Venice."

The prince looked astonished and turned to the Venetian ambassador, who smiled, and whispered to him for ten minutes.

"It's a pity," said the prince, kindly, "that you cannot claim the protection of any ambassador."

At these words a nobleman of colossal stature stepped forward and said I could claim his protection, as my whole family, myself included, had served the prince his master. He spoke the truth, for he was the ambassador of Saxony.

"That is Count Vitzthum," said the prince. "Write to the empress, and I will forward your petition immediately. If there is any delay in the answer, go to the count; you will be safe with him, until you like to leave Vienna."

In the meanwhile the prince ordered writing materials to be brought me, and he and his guests passed into the dining-hall.

I give here a copy of the petition, which I composed in less than ten minutes. I made a fair copy for the Venetian ambassador to send home to the Senate:

"MADAM,—I am sure that if, as your royal and imperial highness were walking in your garden, an insect appealed plaintively to you not to crush it, you would turn aside, and so avoid doing the poor creature any hurt.

"I, madam, am an insect, and I beg of you that you will order M. Statthalter Schrotembach to delay crushing me with your majesty's slipper for a week. Possibly, after that time has elapsed, your majesty will not only prevent his crushing me, but will deprive him of that slipper, which was only meant to be the terror of rogues, and not of an humble Venetian, who is an honest man, though he escaped from The Leads.

"In profound submission to your majesty's will,
  "I remain,
      "CASANOVA.

"Given at Vienna, January 21st, 1769."

When I had finished the petition, I made a fair draft of it, and sent it in to the prince, who sent it back to me telling me that he would place it in the empress's hands immediately, but that he would be much obliged by my making a copy for his own use.

I did so, and gave both copies to the valet de chambre, and went my way. I trembled like a paralytic, and was afraid that my anger might get me into difficulty. By way of calming myself, I wrote out in the style of a manifesto the narrative I had given to the vile Schrotembach, and which that unworthy magistrate had refused to return to me.

At seven o'clock Count Vitzthum came into my room. He greeted me in a friendly manner and begged me to tell him the story of the girl I had gone to see, on the promise of the Latin quatrain referring to her accommodating disposition. I gave him the address and copied out the verses, and he said that was enough to convince an enlightened judge that I had been slandered; but he, nevertheless, was very doubtful whether justice would be done me.

"What! shall I be obliged to leave Vienna to-morrow?"

"No, no, the empress cannot possibly refuse you the week's delay."

"Why not?"

"Oh! no one could refuse such an appeal as that. Even the prince could not help smiling as he was reading it in his cold way. After reading it he passed it on to me, and then to the Venetian ambassador, who asked him if he meant to give it to the empress as it stood. 'This petition,' replied the prince, 'might be sent to God, if one knew the way;' and forthwith he ordered one of his secretaries to fold it up and see that it was delivered. We talked of you for the rest of dinner, and I had the pleasure of hearing the Venetian ambassador say that no one could discover any reason for your imprisonment under the Leads. Your duel was also discussed, but on that point we only knew what has appeared in the newspapers. Oblige me by giving me a copy of your petition; that phrase of Schrotembach and the slipper pleased me vastly."

I copied out the document, and gave it him with a copy of my manifesto. Before he left me the count renewed the invitation to take refuge with him, if I did not hear from the empress before the expiration of the twenty-four hours.

At ten o'clock I had a visit from the Comte de la Perouse, the Marquis de las Casas, and Signor Uccelli, the secretary of the Venetian embassy. The latter came to ask for a copy of my petition for his chief. I promised he should have it, and I also sent a copy of my manifesto. The only thing which rather interfered with the dignity of this latter piece, and gave it a somewhat comic air, were the four Latin verses, which might make people imagine that, after enjoying the girl as Hebe, I had gone in search of her as Ganymede. This was not the case, but the empress understood Latin and was familiar with mythology, and if she had looked on it in the light I have mentioned I should have been undone. I made six copies of the two documents before I went to bed; I was quite tired out, but the exertion had somewhat soothed me. At noon the next day, young Hasse (son of the chapel-master and of the famous Trustina), secretary of legation to Count Vitzthum, came to tell me from the ambassador that nobody would attack me in my own house, nor in my carriage if I went abroad, but that it would be imprudent to go out on foot. He added that his chief would have the pleasure of calling on me at seven o'clock. I begged M. Hasse to let me have all this in writing, and after he had written it out he left me.

Thus the order to leave Vienna had been suspended; it must have been done by the sovereign.

"I have no time to lose," said I to myself, "I shall have justice done me, my assassins will be condemned, my purse will be returned with the two hundred ducats in it, and not in the condition in which it was shewn to me by the infamous Schrotembach, who will be punished by dismissal, at least."

Such were my castles in Spain; who has not built such? 'Quod nimis miseri volunt hoc facile credunt', says Seneca. The wish is father to the thought.

Before sending my manifesto to the empress, Prince Kaunitz, and to all the ambassadors, I thought it would be well to call on the Countess of Salmor, who spoke to the sovereign early and late. I had had a letter of introduction for her.

She greeted me by saying that I had better give up wearing my arm in a sling, as it looked as if I were a charlatan; my arm must be well enough after nine months.

I was extremely astonished by this greeting, and replied that if it were not necessary I should not wear a sling, and that I was no charlatan.

"However," I added, "I have come to see you on a different matter."

"Yes, I know, but I will have nothing to do with it. You are all as bad as Tomatis."

I gave a turn round and left the room without taking any further notice of her. I returned home feeling overwhelmed by the situation. I had been robbed and insulted by a band of thorough-paced rascals; I could do nothing, justice was denied me, and now

I had been made a mock of by a worthless countess. If I had received such an insult from a man I would have soon made him feel the weight of one arm at all events. I could not bear my arm without a sling for an hour; pain and swelling set in immediately. I was not perfectly cured till twenty months after the duel.

Count Vitzthum came to see me at seven o'clock. He said the empress had told Prince Kaunitz that Schrotembach considered my narrative as pure romance. His theory was that I had held a bank at faro with sharpers' cards, and had dealt with both hands the arm in the sling being a mere pretence. I had then been taken in the act by one of the gamesters, and my unjust gains had been very properly taken from me. My detector had then handed over my purse, containing forty ducats, to the police, and the money had of course been confiscated. The empress had to choose between believing Schrotembach and dismissing him; and she was not inclined to do the latter, as it would be a difficult matter to find him a successor in his difficult and odious task of keeping Vienna clear of human vermin.

"This is what Prince Kaunitz asked me to tell you. But you need not be afraid of any violence, and you can go when you like."

"Then I am to be robbed of two hundred ducats with impunity. The empress might at least reimburse me if she does nothing more. Please to ask the prince whether I can ask the sovereign to give me that satisfaction; the least I can demand."

"I will tell him what you say."

"If not, I shall leave; for what can I do in a town where I can only drive, and where the Government keeps assassins in its pay?"

"You are right. We are all sure that Pocchini has calumniated you. The girl who recites Latin verses is well known, but none know her address. I must advise you not to publish your tale as long as you are in Vienna, as it places Schrotembach in a very bad light, and you see the empress has to support him in the exercise of his authority."

"I see the force of your argument, and I shall have to devour my anger. I will leave Vienna as soon as the washerwoman sends home my linen, but I will have the story printed in all its black injustice."

"The empress is prejudiced against you, I don't know by whom."

"I know, though; it is that infernal old hag, Countess Salmor."

The next day I received a letter from Count Vitzthum, in which he said that Prince Kaunitz advised me to forget the two hundred ducats, that the girl and her so-called mother had left Vienna to all appearance, as someone had gone to the address and had failed to find her.

I saw that I could do nothing, and resolved to depart in peace, and afterwards to publish the whole story and to hang Pocchini with my own hands when next I met him. I did neither the one nor the other.

About that time a young lady of the Salis de Coire family arrived at Vienna without any companion. The imperial hangman

Schrotembach, ordered her to leave Vienna in two days. She replied that she would leave exactly when she felt inclined. The magistrate consigned her to imprisonment in a convent, and she was there still when I left. The emperor went to see her, and the empress, his mother, asked him what he thought of her. His answer was, "I thought her much more amusing than Schrotembach."

Undoubtedly, every man worthy of the name longs to be free, but who is really free in this world? No one. The philosopher, perchance, may be accounted so, but it is at the cost of too precious sacrifices at the phantom shrine of Liberty.

I left the use of my suite of rooms, for which I had paid a month in advance, to Campioni, promising to wait for him at Augsburg, where the Law alone is supreme. I departed alone carrying with me the bitter regret that I had not been able to kill the monster, whose despotism had crushed me. I stopped at Linz on purpose to write to Schrotembach even a more bitter letter than that which I had written to the Duke of Wurtemburg in 1760. I posted it myself, and had it registered so as to be sure of its reaching the scoundrel to whom it had been addressed. It was absolutely necessary for me to write this letter, for rage that has no vent must kill at last. From Linz I had a three days' journey to Munich, where I called on Count Gaetan Zavoicki, who died at Dresden seven years ago. I had known him at Venice when he was in want, and I had happily been useful to him. On my relating the story of the robbery that had been committed on me, he no doubt imagined I was in want, and gave me twenty-five louis. To tell the truth it was much less than what I had given him at Venice, and if he had looked upon his action as paying back a debt we should not have been quits; but as I had never wished him to think that I had lent, not given him money, I received the present gratefully. He also gave me a letter for Count Maximilian Lamberg, marshal at the court of the Prince-Bishop of Augsburg, whose acquaintance I had the honour of having.

There was no theatre then in Augsburg, but there were masked balls in which all classes mingled freely. There were also small parties where faro was played for small stakes. I was tired of the pleasure, the misfortune, and the griefs I had had in three capitals, and I resolved to spend four months in the free city of Augsburg, where strangers have the same privileges as the canons. My purse was slender, but with the economical life I led I had nothing to fear on that score. I was not far from Venice, where a hundred ducats were always at my service if I wanted them. I played a little and waged war against the sharpers who have become more numerous of late than the dupes, as there are also more doctors than patients. I also thought of getting a mistress, for what is life without love? I had tried in vain to retrace Gertrude; the engraver was dead, and no one knew what had become of his daughter.

Two or three days before the end of the carnival I went to a hirer of carriages, as I had to go to a ball at some distance from the town. While the horses were being put in, I entered the room to warm my hands, for the weather was very cold. A girl came up and asked me if I would drink a glass of wine.

"No," said I; and on the question being repeated, repeated the monosyllable somewhat rudely. The girl stood still and began to laugh, and I was about to turn angrily away when she said,—

"I see you do not remember me?"

I looked at her attentively, and at last I discovered beneath her unusually ugly features the lineaments of Anna Midel, the maid in the engraver's house.

"You remind me of Anna Midel," said I.

"Alas, I was Anna Midel once. I am no longer an object fit for love, but that is your fault."

"Mine?"

"Yes; the four hundred florins you gave me made Count Fugger's coachman marry me, and he not only abandoned me but gave me a disgusting disease, which was like to have been my death. I recovered my health, but I never shall recover my good looks."

"I am very sorry to hear all this; but tell me what has become of Gertrude?"

"Then you don't know that you are going to a ball at her house to-night?"

"Her house?"

"Yes. After her father's death she married a well-to-do and respectable man, and I expect you will be pleased with the entertainment."

"Is she pretty still?"

"She is just as she used to be, except that she is six years older and has had children."

"Is she gallant?"

"I don't think so."

Anna had spoken the truth. Gertrude was pleased to see me, and introduced me to her husband as one of her father's old lodgers, and I had altogether a pleasant welcome; but, on sounding her, I found she entertained those virtuous sentiments which might have been expected under the circumstances.

Campioni arrived at Augsburg at the beginning of Lent. He was in company with Binetti, who was going to Paris. He had completely despoiled his wife, and had left her for ever. Campioni told me that no one at Vienna doubted my story in the slightest degree. Pocchini and the Sclav had disappeared a few days after my departure, and the Statthalter had incurred a great deal of odium by his treatment of me. Campioni spent a month with me, and then went on to London.

I called on Count Lamberg and his countess, who, without being beautiful, was an epitome of feminine charm and amiability. Her name before marriage was Countess Dachsberg. Three months after my arrival, this lady, who was enciente, but did not think her time was due, went with Count Fugger, dean of the chapter, to a party of pleasure at an inn three quarters of a league from Augsburg. I was present; and in the course of the meal she was taken with such violent pains that she feared she would be delivered on the spot. She did not like to tell the noble canon, and thinking that I was more likely to be acquainted with such emergencies she came up to me and told me all. I ordered the coachman to put in his horses instantly, and when the coach was ready I took up the countess and carried her to it. The canon followed us in blank astonishment, and asked me what was the matter. I told him to bid the coachman drive fast and not to spare his horses. He did so, but he asked again what was the matter.

"The countess will be delivered of a child if we do not make haste."

I thought I should be bound to laugh, in spite of my sympathies for the poor lady's pains, when I saw the dean turn green and white and purple, and look as if he were going into a fit, as he realized that the countess might be delivered before his eyes in his own carriage. The poor man looked as grievously tormented as St. Laurence on his gridiron. The bishop was at Plombieres; they would write and tell him! It would be in all the papers! "Quick! coachman, quick!"

We got to the castle before it was too late. I carried the lady into her rook, and they ran for a surgeon and a midwife. It was no good, however, for in five minutes the count came out and said the countess had just been happily delivered. The dean looked as if a weight had been taken off his mind; however, he took the precaution of having himself blooded.

I spent an extremely pleasant four months at Augsburg, supping twice or thrice a week at Count Lamberg's. At these suppers I made the acquaintance of a very remarkable man—Count Thura and Valsamina, then a page in the prince-bishop's household, now Dean of Ratisbon. He was always at the count's, as was also Dr. Algardi, of Bologna, the prince's physician and a delightful man.

I often saw at the same house a certain Baron Sellenthin, a Prussian officer, who was always recruiting for his master at Augsburg. He was a pleasant man, somewhat in the Gascon style, soft-spoken, and an expert gamester. Five or six years ago I had a letter from him dated Dresden, in which he said that though he was old, and had married a rich wife, he repented of having married at all. I should say the same if I had ever chanced to marry.

During my stay at Augsburg several Poles, who had left their country on account of the troubles, came to see me. Amongst others was Rzewuski, the royal Prothonotary, whom I had known at St. Petersburg as the lover of poor Madame Langlade.

"What a diet! What plots! What counterplots! What misfortunes!" said this honest Pole, to me. "Happy are they who have nothing to do with it!"

He was going to Spa, and he assured me that if I followed him I should find Prince Adam's sister, Tomatis, and Madame Catai, who had become the manager's wife. I determined to go to Spa, and to take measures so that I might go there with three or four hundred ducats in my purse. To this intent I wrote to Prince Charles of Courland, who was at Venice, to send me a hundred ducats, and in my letter I gave him an infallible receipt for the philosopher's stone. The letter containing this vast secret was not in cypher, so I advised him to burn it after he had read it, assuring him that I possessed a copy. He did not do so, and it was taken to Paris with his order papers when he was sent to the Bastile.

If it had not been for the Revolution my letter would never have seen the light. When the Bastille was destroyed, my letter was found and printed with other curious compositions, which were afterwards translated into German and English. The ignorant fools that abound in the land where my fate wills that I should write down the chief events of my long and troublous life—these fools, I say, who are naturally my sworn foes (for the ass lies not down with the horse), make this letter an article of accusation against me, and think they can stop my mouth by telling me that the letter has been translated into German, and remains to my eternal shame. The ignorant Bohemians are astonished when I tell them that I regard the letter as redounding to my glory, and that if their ears were not quite so long their blame would be turned into praise.

I do not know whether my letter has been correctly translated, but since it has become public property I shall set it down here in homage to truth, the only god I adore. I have before me an exact copy of the original written in Augsburg in the year 1767, and we are now in the year 1798.

It runs as follows:

"MY LORD,—I hope your highness will either burn this letter after reading it, or else preserve it with the greatest care. It will be better, however, to make a copy in cypher, and to burn the original. My attachment to you is not my only motive in writing; I confess my interest is equally concerned. Allow me to say that I do not wish your highness to esteem me alone for any qualities you may have observed in me; I wish you to become my debtor by the inestimable secret I am going to confide to you. This secret relates to the making of gold, the only thing of which your highness stands in need. If you had been miserly by nature you would be rich now; but you are generous, and will be poor all your days if you do not make use of my secret.

"Your highness told me at Riga that you would like me to give you the secret by which I transmuted iron into copper; I never did so, but now I shall teach you how to make a much more marvellous transmutation. I should point out to you, however, that you are not at present in a suitable place for the operation, although all the materials are easily procurable. The operation necessitates my presence for the construction of a furnace, and for the great care necessary, far the least mistake will spoil all. The transmutation of Mars is an easy and merely mechanical process, but that of gold is philosophical in the highest degree. The gold produced will be equal to that used in the Venetian sequins. You must reflect, my lord, that I am giving you information which will permit you to dispense with me, and you must also reflect that I am confiding to you my life and my liberty.

"The step I am taking should insure your life-long protection, and should raise you above that prejudice which is entertained against the general mass of alchemists. My vanity would be wounded if you refuse to distinguish me from the common herd of operators. All I ask you is that you will wait till we meet before undertaking the process. You cannot do it by yourself, and if you employ any other person but myself, you will betray the secret. I must tell you that, using the same materials, and by the addition of mercury and nitre, I made the tree of projection for the Marchioness d'Urfe and the Princess of Anhalt. Zerbst calculated the profit as fifty per cent. My fortune would have been made long ago, if I had found a prince with the control of a mint whom I could trust. Your character enables me to confide in you. However, we will come to the point.

"You must take four ounces of good silver, dissolve in aqua fortis, precipitate secundum artem with copper, then wash in lukewarm water to separate the acids; dry, mix with half an ounce of sal ammoniac, and place in a suitable vessel. Afterwards you must take a pound of alum, a pound of Hungary crystals, four ounces of verdigris, four ounces of cinnabar, and two ounces of sulphur. Pulverise and mix, and place in a retort of such size that the above matters will only half fill it. This retort must be placed over a furnace with four draughts, for the heat must be raised to the fourth degree. At first your fire must be slow so as to extract the gross phlegm of the matter, and when the spirit begins to appear, place the receiver under the retort, and Luna with the ammoniac salts will appear in it. All the joinings must be luted with the Philosophical Luting, and as the spirit comes, so regulate your furnace, but do not let it pass the third degree of heat.

"So soon as the sublimation begins then boldly open your forth vent, but take heed that that which is sublimed pass not into the receiver where is your Luna, and so you must shut, the mouth of the retort closely, and keep it so for twenty-four hours, and then take off your fastenings, and allow the distillation to go on. Then you must increase your fire so that the spirits may pass, over, until the matter in the retort is quite desiccated. After this operation has been performed three times, then you shall see, the gold appear in the retort. Then draw it forth and melt it, adding your corpus perfectum. Melt with it two ounces of gold, then lay it in water, and you shall find four ounces of pure gold.

"Such my lord, is the gold mine for your mint of Mitau, by which, with the assistance of a manager and four men, you can assure yourself a revenue of a thousand ducats a week, and double, and quadruple that sum, if your highness chooses to increase the men and the furnaces. I ask your highness to make me your manager. But remember it must be a State secret, so burn this letter, and if your highness would give me any reward in advance, I only ask you to give me your affection and esteem. I shall be happy if I have reason to believe that my master will also be my friend. My life, which this letter places in your power, is ever at your service, and I know not what I shall do if I ever have cause to repent having disclosed my secret. I have the honour to be, etc."

In whatever language this letter may have been translated, if its sense run not as above, it is not my letter, and I am ready to give the lie to all the Mirabeaus in the world. I have been called an exile, but wrongfully, for a man who has to leave a country by virtue of a 'lettre de cachet' is no exile. He is forced to obey a despotic monarch who looks upon his kingdom as his house, and turns out of doors anyone who meets with his displeasure.

As soon as my purse swelled to a respectable size, I left Augsburg, The date of my departure was June 14th, 1767. I was at Ulm when a courier of the Duke of Wurtemburg's passed through the town with the news that his highness would arrive from Venice in the course of five or six days. This courier had a letter for me. It had been entrusted to him by Prince Charles of Courland, who had told the courier that he would find me at the "Hotel du Raisin," in Augsburg. As it happened, I had left the day before, but knowing the way by which I had gone he caught me up at Ulm. He gave me the letter and asked me if I were the same Casanova who had been placed under arrest and had escaped, on account of some gambling dispute with three officers. As I was never an adept in concealing the truth, I replied in the affirmative. A Wurtemburg officer who was standing beside us observed to me in a friendly manner that he was at Stuttgart at the time, and that most people concurred in blaming the three officers for their conduct in the matter.

Without making any reply I read the letter, which referred to our private affairs, but as I was reading it I resolved to tell a little lie— one of those lies which do nobody any harm.

"Well, sir," I said to the officer, "his highness, your sovereign, has listened to reason at last, and this letter informs me of a reparation which is in every way satisfactory. The duke has created me his private secretary, with a salary of twelve hundred a year. But I have waited for it a long time. God knows what has become of the three officers!"

"They are all at Louisburg, and—— -is now a colonel."

"Well, they will be surprised to hear my news, and they will hear it to-morrow, for I am leaving this place in an hour. If they are at Louisburg, I shall have a triumph; but I am sorry not to be able to accompany you, however we shall see each other the day after tomorrow."

I had an excellent night, and awoke with the beautiful idea of going to Louisburg, not to fight the three officers but to frighten them, triumph over them, and to enjoy a pleasant vengeance for the injury they had done me. I should at the same time see a good many old friends; there was Madame Toscani, the duke's mistress; Baletti, and Vestri, who had married a former mistress of the duke's. I had sounded the depths of the human heart, and knew I had nothing to fear. The duke was on the point of returning, and nobody would dream of impugning the truth of my story. When he actually did arrive he would not find me, for as soon as the courier announced his approach I should go away, telling everybody that I had orders to precede his highness, and everybody would be duped.

I never had so pleasant an idea before. I was quite proud of it, and I should have despised myself if I had failed to carry it into effect. It would be my vengeance on the duke, who could not have forgotten the terrible letter I had written him; for princes do not forget small injuries as they forget great services.

I slept badly the following night, my anxiety was so great, and I reached Louisburg and gave my name at the town gates, without the addition of my pretended office, for my jest must be matured by degrees. I went to stay at the posting-inn, and just as I was asking for the address of Madame Toscani, she and her husband appeared on the scene. They both flung their arms around my neck, and overwhelmed me with compliments on my wounded arm and the victory I had achieved.

"What victory?"

"Your appearance here has filled the hearts of all your friends with joy."

"Well, I certainly am in the duke's service, but how did you find it out?"

"It's the common talk. The courier who gave you the letter has spread it all abroad, and the officer who was present and arrived here yesterday morning confirmed it. But you cannot imagine the consternation of your three foes. However, we are afraid that you will have some trouble with them, as they have kept your letter of defiance given from Furstenberg."

"Why didn't they meet me, then?"

"Two of them could not go, and the third arrived too late."

"Very good. If the duke has no objection I shall be happy to meet them one after another, not three all at once. Of course, the duel must be with pistols; a sword duel is out of the question with my arm in a sling."

"We will speak of that again. My daughter wants to make peace before the duke comes, and you had better consent to arrangements, for there are three of them, and it isn't likely that you could kill the whole three one after the other."

"Your daughter must have grown into a beauty."

"You must stop with us this evening; you will see her, for she is no longer the duke's mistress. She is going to get married."

"If your daughter can bring about an arrangement I would gladly fall in with it, provided it is an honourable one for me."

"How is it that you are wearing the sling after all these months?"

"I am quite cured, and yet my arm swells as soon as I let it swing loose. You shall see it after dinner, for you must dine with me if you want me to sup with you."

Next came Vestri, whom I did not know, accompanied by my beloved Baletti. With them was an officer who was in love with Madame Toscani's second daughter, and another of their circle, with whom I was also unacquainted. They all came to congratulate me on my honourable position in the duke's service. Baletti was quite overcome with delight. The reader will recollect that he was my chief assistant in my escape from Stuttgart, and that I was once going to marry his sister. Baletti was a fine fellow, and the duke was very fond of him. He had a little country house, with a spare room, which he begged me to accept, as he said he was only too proud that the duke should know him as my best friend. When his highness came, of course I would have an apartment in the palace. I accepted; and as it was still early, we all went to see the young Toscani. I had loved her in Paris before her beauty had reached its zenith, and she was naturally proud to shew me how beautiful she had become. She shewed me her house and her jewels, told me the story of her amours with the duke, of her breaking with him on account of his perpetual infidelities, and of her marriage with a man she despised, but who was forced on her by her position.

At dinner-time we all went to the inn, where we met the offending colonel; he was the first to take off his hat, we returned the salute, and he passed on his way.

The dinner was a pleasant one, and when it was over I proceeded to take up my quarters with Baletti. In the evening we went to Madame Toscani's, where I saw two girls of ravishing beauty, Madame Toscani's daughter and Vestri's wife, of whom the duke had had two children. Madame Vestri was a handsome woman, but her wit and the charm of her manner enchanted me still more. She had only one fault—she lisped.

There was a certain reserve about the manner of Mdlle. Toscani, so I chiefly addressed myself to Madame Vestri, whose husband was not jealous, for he neither cared for her nor she for him. On the day of my arrival the manager had distributed the parts of a little play which was to be given in honour of the duke's arrival. It had been written by a local author, in hopes of its obtaining the favour of the Court for him.

After supper the little piece was discussed. Madame Vestri played the principal part, which she was prevailed upon to recite.

"Your elocution is admirable, and your expression full of spirit," I observed; "but what a pity it is that you do not pronounce the dentals."

The whole table scouted my opinion.

"It's a beauty, not a defect," said they. "It makes her acting soft and delicate; other actresses envy her the privilege of what you call a defect."

I made no answer, but looked at Madame Vestri.

"Do you think I am taken in by all that?" said she.

"I think you are much too sensible to believe such nonsense."

"I prefer a man to say honestly, 'what a pity,' than to hear all that foolish flattery. But I am sorry to say that there is no remedy for the defect."

"No remedy?"

"No."

"Pardon me, I have an infallible remedy for your complaint. You shall give me a good hearty blow if I do not make you read the part perfectly by to-morrow, but if I succeed in making you read it as your husband, for example's sake, might read it you shall permit me to give you a tender embrace."

"Very good; but what must I do?"

"You must let me weave a spell over your part, that is all. Give it to me. To-morrow morning at nine o'clock I will bring it to you to get my blow or my kiss, if your husband has no objection."

"None whatever; but we do not believe in spells."

"You are right, in a general way; but mine will not fail."

"Very good."

Madame Vestri left me the part, and the conversation turned on other subjects. I was condoled with on my swollen hand, and I told the story of my duel. Everybody seemed to delight in entertaining me and feasting me, and I went back to Baletti's in love with all the ladies, but especially with Madame Vestri and Mdlle. Toscani.

Baletti had a beautiful little girl of three years old.

"How did you get that angel?" I asked.

"There's her mother; and, as a proof of my hospitality, she shall sleep with you to-night."

"I accept your generous offer; but let it be to-morrow night."

"And why not to-night?"

"Because I shall be engaged all night in weaving my spell."

"What do you mean? I thought that was a joke."

"No, I am quite serious."

"Are you a little crazy?"

"You shall see. Do you go to bed, and leave me a light and writing materials."

I spent six hours in copying out the part, only altering certain phrases. For all words in which the letter r appeared I substituted another. It was a tiresome task, but I longed to embrace Madame Vestri before her husband. I set about my task in the following manner:

The text ran:

"Les procedes de cet homme m'outragent et me deseparent, je dois penser a me debarrasser."

For this I substituted:

"Cet homme a des facons qui m'offensent et me desolent, il faut que je m'en defasse;" and so on throughout the piece.

When I had finished I slept for three hours, and then rose and dressed. Baletti saw my spell, and said I had earned the curses of the young author, as Madame Vestri would no doubt make him write all parts for her without using the letter 'r'; and, indeed, that was just what she did.

I called on the actress and found her getting up. I gave her the part, and as soon as she saw what I had done she burst out into exclamations of delight; and calling her husband shewed him my contrivance, and said she would never play a part with an 'r' in it again. I promised to copy them all out, and added that I had spent the whole night in amending the present part. "The whole night! Come and take your reward, for you are cleverer than any sorcerer. We must have the author to dinner, and I shall make him promise to write all my parts without the 'r', or the duke will not employ him. Indeed, I don't wonder the duke has made you his secretary. I never thought it would be possible to do what you have done; but I suppose it was very difficult?"

"Not at all. If I were a pretty woman with the like defect I should take care to avoid all words with an 'r; in them."

"Oh, that would be too much trouble."

"Let us bet again, for a box or a kiss, that you can spend a whole day without using an 'r'. Let us begin now."

"All in good time," said she, "but we won't have any stake, as I think you are too greedy."

The author came to dinner, and was duly attacked by Madame Vestri. She began by saying that it was an author's duty to be polite to actresses, and if any of them spoke with a lisp the least he could do was to write their parts without the fatal letter.

The young author laughed, and said it could not be done without spoiling the style. Thereupon Madame Vestri gave him my version of her part, telling him to read it, and to say on his conscience whether the style had suffered. He had to confess that my alterations were positive improvements, due to the great richness of the French language. And he was right, for there is no language in the world that can compare in copiousness of expression with the French.

This trifling subject kept us merry, but Madame Vestri expressed a devout wish that all authors would do for her what I had done. At Paris, where I heard her playing well and lisping terribly, she did not find the authors so obliging, but she pleased the people. She asked me if I would undertake to recompose Zaire, leaving out the r's.

"Ah!" said I, "considering that it would have to be in verse, and in Voltairean verse, I would rather not undertake the task."

With a view to pleasing the actress the young author asked me how I would tell her that she was charming without using an 'r'.

"I should say that she enchanted me, made me in an ecstasy, that she is unique."

She wrote me a letter, which I still keep, in which the 'r' does not appear. If I could have stayed at Stuttgart, this device of mine might have won me her favours; but after a week of feasting and triumph the courier came one morning at ten o'clock and announced that his highness, the duke, would arrive at four.

As soon as I heard the news I told Baletti with the utmost coolness that I thought it would be only polite to meet my lord, and swell his train on his entry into Louisburg; and as I wished to meet him at a distance of two stages I should have to go at once. He thought my idea an excellent one, and went to order post-horses immediately; but when he saw me packing up all my belongings into my trunk, he guessed the truth and applauded the jest. I embraced him and confessed my hardihood. He was sorry to lose me, but he laughed when he thought of the feelings of the duke and of the three officers when they found out the trick. He promised to write to me at Mannheim, where I had decided on spending a week to see my beloved Algardi, who was in the service of the Elector. I had also letters for M. de Sickirigen and Baron Becker, one of the Elector's ministers.

When the horses were put in I embraced Baletti, his little girl, and his pretty housekeeper, and ordered the postillion to drive to Mannheim.

When we reached Mannheim I heard that the Court was at Schwetzingen, and I bade the postillion drive on. I found everyone I had expected to see. Algardi had got married, M. de Sickingen was soliciting the position of ambassador to Paris, and Baron Becker introduced me to the Elector. Five or six days after my arrival died Prince Frederic des Deux Ponts, and I will here relate an anecdote I heard the day before he died.

Dr. Algardi had attended on the prince during his last illness. I was supping with Veraci, the poet-laureate, on the eve of the prince's death, and in the course of supper Algardi came in.

"How is the prince?" said I.

"The poor prince—he cannot possibly live more than twenty-four hours."

"Does he know it?"

"No, he still hopes. He grieved me to the heart by bidding me tell him the whole truth; he even bade me give my word of honour that I was speaking the truth. Then he asked me if he were positively in danger of death."

"And you told him the truth?"

"Certainly not. I told him his sickness was undoubtedly a mortal one, but that with the help of nature and art wonders might be worked."

"Then you deceived him, and told a lie?"

"I did not deceive him; his recovery comes under the category of the possible. I did not want to leave him in despair, for despair would most certainly kill him."

"Yes, yes; but you will confess that you told him a lie and broke your word of honour."

"I told no lie, for I know that he may possibly be cured."

"Then you lied just now?"

"Not at all, for lie will die to-morrow."

"It seems to me that your reasoning is a little Jesuitical."

"No, it is not. My duty was to prolong my patient's life and to spare him a sentence which would most certainly have shortened it, possibly by several hours; besides, it is not an absolute impossibility that he should recover, therefore I did not lie when I told him that he might recover, nor did I lie just now when I gave it as my opinion (the result of my experience) that he would die to-morrow. I would certainly wager a million to one that he will die to-morrow, but I would not wager my life."

"You are right, and yet for all that you deceived the poor man; for his intention in asking you the question was not to be told a commonplace which he knew as well as you, but to learn your true opinion as to his life or death. But again I agree with you that as his physician you were quite right not to shorten his few remaining hours by telling him the terrible truth."

After a fortnight I left Schwetzingen, leaving some of my belongings under the care of Veraci the poet, telling him I would call for them some day; but I never came, and after a lapse of thirty-one years Veraci keeps them still. He was one of the strangest poets I have ever met. He affected eccentricity to make himself notorious, and opposed the great Metastasio in everything, writing unwieldy verses which he said gave more scope for the person who set them to music. He had got this extravagant notion from Jumelli.

I traveled to Mayence and thence I sailed to Cologne, where I looked forward to the pleasure of meeting with the burgomaster's wife who disliked General Kettler, and had treated me so well seven years ago. But that was not the only reason which impelled me to visit that odious town. When I was at Dresden I had read in a number of the Cologne Gazette that "Master Casanova has returned to Warsaw only to be sent about his business again. The king has heard some stories of this famous adventurer, which compel him to forbid him his Court."

I could not stomach language of this kind, and I resolved to pay Jacquet, the editor, a visit, and now my time had come.

I made a hasty dinner and then called on the burgomaster, whom I found sitting at table with his fair Mimi. They welcomed me warmly, and for two hours I told them the story of my adventures during the last seven years. Mimi had to go out, and I was asked to dine with them the next day.

I thought she looked prettier than ever, and my imagination promised me some delicious moments with her. I spent an anxious and impatient night, and called on my Amphitryon at an early hour to have an opportunity of speaking to his dear companion. I found her alone, and began with an ardent caress which she gently repelled, but her face froze my passion in its course.

"Time is an excellent doctor," said she, "and it has cured me of a passion which left behind it the sting of remorse."

"What! The confessional . . . ."

"Should only serve as a place wherein to confess our sins of the past, and to implore grace to sin no more."

"May the Lord save me from repentance, the only source of which is a prejudice! I shall leave Cologne to-morrow."

"I do not tell you to go."

"If there is no hope, it is no place for me. May I hope?"

"Never."

She was delightful at table, but I was gloomy and distracted. At seven o'clock next day I set out, and as soon as I had passed the Aix la Chapelle Gate, I told the postillion to stop and wait for me. I then walked to Jacquet's, armed with a pistol and a cane, though I only meant to beat him.

The servant shewed me into the room where he was working by himself. It was on the ground floor, and the door was open for coolness' sake.

He heard me coming in and asked what he could do for me.

"You scoundrelly journalist." I replied, "I am the adventurer Casanova whom you slandered in your miserable sheet four months ago."

So saying I directed my pistol at his head, with my left hand, and lifted my cane with my right. But the wretched scribbler fell on his knees before me with clasped hands and offered to shew me the signed letter he had received from Warsaw, which contained the statements he had inserted in his paper.

"Where is this letter?"

"You shall have it in a moment."

I made way for him to search, but I locked and bolted the door to prevent his escaping. The man trembled like a leaf and began to look for the letter amongst his Warsaw correspondence, which was in a disgraceful state of confusion. I shewed him the date of the article in the paper, but the letter could not be found; and at the end of an hour he fell down again on his knees, and told me to do what I would to him. I gave him a kick and told him to get up and follow me. He made no reply, and followed me bareheaded till he saw me get into my chaise and drive off, and I have no doubt he gave thanks to God for his light escape. In the evening, I reached Aix-la-Chapelle, where I found Princess Lubomirska, General Roniker, several other distinguished Poles, Tomatis and his wife, and many Englishmen of my acquaintance.

CHAPTER II

My Stay at Spa—The Blow—The Sword—Della Croce—Charlotte;
Her Lying-in and Death—A Lettre de Cachet Obliges Me to Leave
Paris in the Course of Twenty-four Hours

All my friends seemed delighted to see me, and I was well pleased
to find myself in such good company. People were on the point of
leaving Aix for Spa. Nearly everyone went, and those who stayed
only did so because lodgings were not to be had at Spa.
Everybody assured me that this was the case, and many had
returned after seeking in vain for a mere garret. I paid no
attention to all this, and told the princess that if she would come
with me I would find some lodging, were it only in my carriage.
We accordingly set out the next day, and got to Spa in good time,
our company consisting of the princess, the prothonotary,
Roniker, and the Tomatis. Everyone except myself had taken
rooms in advance, I alone knew not where to turn. I got out and
prepared for the search, but before going along the streets I went
into a shop and bought a hat, having lost mine on the way. I
explained my situation to the shopwoman, who seemed to take an
interest in me, and began speaking to her husband in Flemish or
Walloon, and finally informed me that if it were only for a few
days she and her husband would sleep in the shop and give up
their room to me. But she said that she had absolutely no room
whatever for my man.

"I haven't got one."

"All the better. Send away your carriage."

"Where shall I send it?"

"I will see that it is housed safely."

"How much am I to pay?"

"Nothing; and if you are not too particular, we should like you to share our meals."

"I accept your offer thankfully."

I went up a narrow staircase, and found myself in a pretty little room with a closet, a good bed, suitable furniture, and everything perfectly neat and clean. I thought myself very lucky, and asked the good people why they would not sleep in the closet rather than the shop, and they replied with one breath that they would be in my way, while their niece would not interfere with me.

This news about the niece was a surprise to me. The closet had no door, and was not much bigger than the bed which it contained; it was, in fact, a mere alcove, without any window.

I must note that my hostess and her husband, both of them from Liège, were perfect models of ugliness.

"It's not within the limits of possibility," I said to myself, "for the niece to be uglier than they, but if they allow her to sleep thus in the same room with the first comer, she must be proof against all temptation."

However, I gave no sign, and did not ask to see the niece for fear of offense, and I went out without opening my trunk. I told them as I went out that I should not be back till after supper, and gave them some money to buy wax candles and night lights.

I went to see the princess with whom I was to sup. All the company congratulated me on my good fortune in finding a lodging. I went to the concert, to the bank at faro, and to the other gaming saloons, and there I saw the so-called Marquis d'Aragon, who was playing at piquet with an old count of the Holy Roman Empire. I was told about the duel he had had three weeks before with a Frenchman who had picked a quarrel with him; the Frenchman had been wounded in the chest, and was still ill. Nevertheless, he was only waiting for his cure to be completed to have his revenge, which he had demanded as he was taken off the field. Such is the way of the French when a duel is fought for a trifling matter. They stop at the first blood, and fight the duel over and over again. In Italy, on the other hand, duels are fought to the death. Our blood burns to fire when our adversary's sword opens a vein. Thus stabbing is common in Italy and rare in France; while duels are common in France, and rare in Italy.

Of all the company at Spa, I was most pleased to see the Marquis Caraccioli, whom I had left in London. His Court had given him leave of absence, and he was spending it at Spa. He was brimful of wit and the milk of human kindness, compassionate for the weaknesses of others, and devoted to youth, no matter of what sex, but he knew well the virtue of moderation, and used all things without abusing them. He never played, but he loved a good gamester and despised all dupes. The worthy marquis was the means of making the fortune of the so-called Marquis d'Aragon by becoming surety for his nobility and bona fides to a wealthy

English widow of fifty, who had taken a fancy to him, and brought him her fortune of sixty thousand pounds sterling. No doubt the widow was taken with the gigantic form and the beautiful title of d'Aragon, for Dragon (as his name really was) was devoid of wit and manners, and his legs, which I suppose he kept well covered, bore disgusting marks of the libertine life he had led. I saw the marquis some time afterwards at Marseilles, and a few years later he purchased two estates at Modena. His wife died in due course, and according to the English law he inherited the whole of her property.

I returned to my lodging in good time, and went to bed without seeing the niece, who was fast asleep. I was waited on by the ugly aunt, who begged me not to take a servant while I remained in her house, for by her account all servants were thieves.

When I awoke in the morning the niece had got up and gone down. I dressed to go to the Wells, and warned my host and hostess that I should have the pleasure of dining with them. The room I occupied was the only place in which they could take their meals, and I was astonished when they came and asked my permission to do so. The niece had gone out, so I had to put my curiosity aside. When I was out my acquaintances pointed out to me the chief beauties who then haunted the Wells. The number of adventurers who flock to Spa during the season is something incredible, and they all hope to make their fortunes; and, as may be supposed, most of them go away as naked as they came, if not more so. Money circulates with great freedom, but principally amongst the gamesters, shop-keepers, money-lenders, and courtezans. The money which proceeds from the gaming-table has three issues: the first and smallest share goes to the Prince-Bishop of Liège; the second and larger portion, to the numerous amateur cheats who frequent the place; and by far the largest of all to the coffers of twelve sharpers, who keep the tables and are authorized by the sovereign.

Thus goes the money. It comes from the pockets of the dupes—poor moths who burn their wings at Spa!

The Wells are a mere pretext for gaming, intriguing, and fortune-hunting. There are a few honest people who go for amusement, and a few for rest and relaxation after the toils of business.

Living is cheap enough at Spa. The table d'hôte is excellent, and only costs a small French crown, and one can get good lodging for the like sum.

I came home at noon having won a score of louis. I went into the shop, intending to go to my room, but I was stopped short by seeing a handsome brunette, of nineteen or twenty, with great black eyes, voluptuous lips, and shining teeth, measuring out ribbon on the counter. This, then, was the niece, whom I had imagined as so ugly. I concealed my surprise and sat down in the shop to gaze at her and endeavour to make her acquaintance. But she hardly seemed to see me, and only acknowledged my presence by a slight inclination of the head. Her aunt came down to say that dinner was ready, and I went upstairs and found the table laid for four. The servant brought in the soup, and then asked me very plainly to give her some money if I wanted any wine, as her master and mistress only drank beer. I was delighted with her freedom, and gave her money to buy two bottles of Burgundy.

The master came up and shewed me a gold repeater with a chain also of gold by a well-known modern maker. He wanted to know how much it was worth.

"Forty louis at the least."

"A gentleman wants me to give him twenty louis for it, on the condition that I return it to-morrow if he brings me twenty-two."

"Then I advise you to accept his offer."

"I haven't got the money."

"I will lend it you with pleasure."

I gave him the twenty Louis, and placed the watch in my jewel-casket. At table the niece sat opposite to me, but I took care not to look at her, and she, like a modest girl, did not say a score of words all through the meal. The meal was an excellent one, consisting of soup, boiled beef, an entree, and a roast. The mistress of the house told me that the roast was in my honour, "for," she said, "we are not rich people, and we only allow ourselves this luxury on a Sunday." I admired her delicacy, and the evident sincerity with which she spoke. I begged my entertainers to help me with my wine, and they accepted the offer, saying they only wished they were rich enough to be able to drink half a bottle a day.

"I thought trade was good with you."

"The stuff is not ours, and we have debts; besides, the expenses are very great. We have sold very little up to now."

"Do you only sell hats?"

"No, we have silk handkerchiefs, Paris stockings, and lace ruffs, but they say everything is too dear."

"I will buy some things for you, and will send all my friends here. Leave it to me; I will see what I can do for you."

"Mercy, fetch down one or two packets of those handkerchiefs and some stockings, large size, for the gentleman has a big leg."

Mercy, as the niece was called, obeyed. I pronounced the handkerchiefs superb and the stockings excellent. I bought a dozen, and I promised them that they should sell out their whole stock. They overwhelmed me with thanks, and promised to put themselves entirely in my hands.

After coffee, which, like the roast, was in my honour, the aunt told her niece to take care to awake me in the morning when she got up. She said she would not fail, but I begged her not to take too much trouble over me, as I was a very heavy sleeper.

In the afternoon I went to an armourer's to buy a brace of pistols, and asked the man if he knew the tradesman with whom I was staying.

"We are cousins-german," he replied.

"Is he rich?"

"Yes, in debts."

"Why?"

"Because he is unfortunate, like most honest people."

"How about his wife?"

"Her careful economy keeps him above water."

"Do you know the niece?"

"Yes; she's a good girl, but very pious. Her silly scruples keep customers away from the shop."

"What do you think she should do to attract customers?"

"She should be more polite, and not play the prude when anyone wants to give her a kiss."

"She is like that, is she?"

"Try her yourself and you will see. Last week she gave an officer a box on the ear. My cousin scolded her, and she wanted to go back to Liege; however, the wife soothed her again. She is pretty enough, don't you think so?"

"Certainly I do, but if she is as cross-grained as you say, the best thing will be to leave her alone."

After what I had heard I made up my mind to change my room, for Mercy had pleased me in such a way that I was sure I should be obliged to pay her a call before long, and I detested Pamelas as heartily as Charpillons.

In the afternoon I took Rzewuski and Roniker to the shop, and they bought fifty ducats' worth of goods to oblige me. The next day the princess and Madame Tomatis bought all the handkerchiefs.

I came home at ten o'clock, and found Mercy in bed as I had done the night before. Next morning the watch was redeemed, and the hatter returned me twenty-two louis. I made him a present of the two louis, and said I should always be glad to lend him money in that way—the profits to be his. He left me full of gratitude.

I was asked to dine with Madame Tomatis, so I told my hosts that I would have the pleasure of supping with them, the costs to be borne by me. The supper was good and the Burgundy excellent, but Mercy refused to taste it. She happened to leave the room for a moment at the close of the meal, and I observed to the aunt that her niece was charming, but it was a pity she was so sad.

"She will have to change her ways, or I will keep her no longer."

"Is she the same with all men?"

"With all."

"Then she has never been in love."

"She says she has not, but I don't believe her."

"I wonder she can sleep so comfortably with a man at a few feet distant."

"She is not afraid."

Mercy came in, bade us good night, and said she would go to bed. I made as if I would give her a kiss, but she turned her back on me, and placed a chair in front of her closet so that I might not see her taking off her chemise. My host and hostess then went to bed, and so did I, puzzling my head over the girl's behaviour which struck me as most extraordinary and unaccountable. However, I slept peacefully, and when I awoke the bird had left the nest. I felt inclined to have a little quiet argument with the girl, and to see what I could make of her; but I saw no chance of my getting an opportunity. The hatter availed himself of my offer of purse to lend money on pledges, whereby he made a good profit. There was no risk for me in the matter, and he and his wife declared that they blessed the day on which I had come to live with them.

On the fifth or sixth day I awoke before Mercy, and only putting on my dressing-gown I came towards her bed. She had a quick ear and woke up, and no sooner did she see me coming towards her than she asked me what I wanted. I sat down on her bed and said gently that I only wanted to wish her a good day and to have a little talk. It was hot weather, and she was only covered by a single sheet; and stretching out one arm I drew her towards me, and begged her to let me give her a kiss. Her resistance made me angry; and passing an audacious hand under the sheet I discovered that she was made like other women; but just as my hand was on the spot, I received a fisticuff on the nose that made me see a thousand stars, and quite extinguished the fire of my concupiscence. The blood streamed from my nose and stained the bed of the furious Mercy. I kept my presence of mind and left her on the spot, as the blow she had given me was but a sample of what I might expect if I attempted reprisals. I washed my face in cold water, and as I was doing so Mercy dressed herself and left the room.

At last my blood ceased to flow, and I saw to my great annoyance that my nose was swollen in such a manner that my face was simply hideous. I covered it up with a handkerchief and sent for the hairdresser to do my hair, and when this was done my landlady brought me up some fine trout, of which I approved; but as I was giving her the money she saw my face and uttered a cry of horror. I told her the whole story, freely acknowledging that I was in the wrong, and begging her to say nothing to her niece. Then heeding not her excuses I went out with my handkerchief before my face, and visited a house which the Duchess of Richmond had left the day before.

Half of the suite she had abandoned had been taken in advance by an Italian marquis; I took the other half, hired a servant, and had my effects transported there from my old lodgings. The tears and supplications of my landlady had no effect whatever upon me, I felt I could not bear the sight of Mercy any longer.

In the house into which I had moved I found an Englishman who said he would bring down the bruise in one hour, and make the discoloration of the flesh disappear in twenty-four. I let him do what he liked and he kept his word. He rubbed the place with spirits of wine and some drug which is unknown to me; but being ashamed to appear in public in the state I was in, I kept indoors for the rest of the day. At noon the distressed aunt brought me my trout, and said that Mercy was cut to the heart to have used me so, and that if I would come back I could do what I liked with her.

"You must feel," I replied, "that if I complied with your request the adventure would become public to the damage of my honour and your business, and your niece would not be able to pass for a devotee any longer."

I made some reflections on the blow she had given the officer, much to the aunt's surprise, for she could not think how I had heard of it; and I shewed her that, after having exposed me to her niece's brutality, her request was extremely out of place. I concluded by saying that I could believe her to be an accomplice in the fact without any great stretch of imagination. This made her burst into tears, and I had to apologize and to promise to continue forwarding her business by way of consolation, and so she left me in a calmer mood. Half an hour afterwards her husband came with twenty-five Louis I had lent him on a gold snuff-box set with diamonds, and proposed that I should lend two hundred Louis on a ring worth four hundred.

"It will be yours," he said, "if the owner does not bring me two hundred and twenty Louis in a week's time."

I had the money and proceeded to examine the stone which seemed to be a good diamond, and would probably weigh six carats as the owner declared. The setting was in gold.

"I consent to give the sum required if the owner is ready to give me a receipt."

"I will do so myself in the presence of witnesses."

"Very good. You shall have the money in the course of an hour; I am going to have the stone taken out first. That will make no difference to the owner, as I shall have it reset at my own expense. If he redeems it, the twenty Louis shall be yours."

"I must ask him whether he has any objection to the stone being taken out."

"Very good, but you can tell him that if he will not allow it to be done he will get nothing for it."

He returned before long with a jeweller who said he would guarantee the stone to be at least two grains over the six carats.

"Have you weighed it?"

"No, but I am quite sure it weighs over six carats."

"Then you can lend the money on it?"

"I cannot command such a sum."

"Can you tell me why the owner objects to the stone being taken out and put in at my expense?"

"No, I can't; but he does object."

"Then he may take his ring somewhere else."

They went away, leaving me well pleased at my refusal, for it was plain that the stone was either false or had a false bottom.

I spent the rest of the day in writing letters and making a good supper. In the morning I was awoke by someone knocking at my door, and on my getting up to open it, what was my astonishment to find Mercy!

I let her in, and went back to bed, and asked her what she wanted with me so early in the morning. She sat down on the bed, and began to overwhelm me with apologies. I replied by asking her why, if it was her principle to fly at her lovers like a tiger, she had slept almost in the same room as myself.

"In sleeping in the closet," said she, "I obeyed my aunt's orders, and in striking you (for which I am very sorry) I was but defending my honour; and I cannot admit that every man who sees me is at liberty to lose his reason. I think you will allow that your duty is to respect, and mine to defend, my honour."

"If that is your line of argument, I acknowledge that you are right; but you had nothing to complain of, for I bore your blow in silence, and by my leaving the house you might know that it was my intention to respect you for the future. Did you come to hear me say this? If so, you are satisfied. But you will not be offended if I laugh at your excuses, for after what you have said I cannot help thinking them very laughable."

"What have I said?"

"That you only did your duty in flattening my nose. If so, do you think it is necessary to apologize for the performance of duty?"

"I ought to have defended myself more gently. But forget everything and forgive me; I will defend myself no more in any way. I am yours and I love you, and I am ready to prove my love."

She could not have spoken more plainly, and as she spoke the last words she fell on me with her face close to mine, which she bedewed with her tears. I was ashamed of such an easy conquest, and I gently withdrew from her embrace, telling her to return after the bruise on my face had disappeared. She left me deeply mortified.

The Italian, who had taken half the suite of rooms, had arrived in the course of the night. I asked his name, and was given a card bearing the name of The Marquis Don Antonio della Croce.

Was it the Croce I knew?

It was very possible.

I asked what kind of an establishment he had, and was informed that the marchioness had a lady's maid, and the marquis a secretary and two servants. I longed to see the nobleman in question.

I had not long to wait, for as soon as he heard that I was his neighbour, he came to see me, and we spent two hours in telling each other our adventures since we had parted in Milan. He had heard that I had made the fortune of the girl he had abandoned, and in the six years that had elapsed he had been travelling all over Europe, engaged in a constant strife with fortune. At Paris and Brussels he had made a good deal of money, and in the latter town he had fallen in love with a young lady of rank, whom her father had shut up in a convent. He had taken her away, and she it was whom he called the Marchioness della Croce, now six months with child.

He made her pass for his wife, because, as he said, he meant to marry her eventually.

"I have fifty thousand francs in gold," said he, "and as much again in jewellery and various possessions. It is my intention to give suppers here and hold a bank, but if I play without correcting the freaks of fortune I am sure to lose." He intended going to Warsaw, thinking I would give him introductions to all my friends there; but he made a mistake, and I did not even introduce him to my Polish friends at Spa. I told him he could easily make their acquaintance by himself, and that I would neither make nor mar with him.

I accepted his invitation to dinner for the same day. His secretary, as he called him, was merely his confederate. He was a clever Veronese named Conti, and his wife was an essential accomplice in Croce's designs.

At noon my friend the hatter came again with the ring, followed by the owner, who looked like a bravo. They were accompanied by the jeweller and another individual. The owner asked me once more to lend him two hundred louis on the ring.

My proper course would have been to beg to be excused, then I should have had no more trouble in the matter; but it was not to be. I wanted to make him see that the objection he made to having the stone taken out was an insuperable obstacle to my lending him the money.

"When the stone is removed," said I, "we shall see what it really is. Listen to my proposal: if it weighs twenty-six grains, I will give you, not two but three hundred louis, but in its present condition I shall give nothing at all."

"You have no business to doubt my word; you insult me by doing so."

"Not at all, I have no intentions of the kind. I simply propose a wager to you. If the stone be found to weigh twenty-six grains, I shall lose two hundred Louis, if it weighs much less you will lose the ring."

"That's a scandalous proposal; it's as much as to tell me that I am a liar."

I did not like the tone with which these words were spoken, and I went up to the chest of drawers where I kept my pistols, and bade him go and leave me in peace.

Just then General Roniker came in, and the owner of the ring told him of the dispute between us. The general looked at the ring, and said to him,—

"If anyone were to give me the ring I should not have the stone taken out, because one should not look a gift horse in the mouth;

but if it came to a question of buying or lending I would not give a crown for it, were the owner an emperor, before the stone was taken out; and I am very much surprised at your refusing to let this be done."

Without a word the knave made for the door, and the ring remained in the hands of my late host.

"Why didn't you give him his ring?" said I.

"Because I have advanced him fifty Louis on it; but if he does not redeem it to-morrow I will have the stone taken out before a judge, and afterwards I shall sell it by auction."

"I don't like the man's manners, and I hope you will never bring anyone to my rooms again."

The affair came to the following conclusion: The impostor did not redeem the ring, and the Liege tradesman had the setting removed. The diamond was found to be placed on a bed of rock crystal, which formed two-thirds of the whole bulk. However, the diamond was worth fifty Louis, and an Englishman bought it. A week afterwards the knave met me as I was walking by myself, and begged me to follow him to place where we should be free from observation, as his sword had somewhat to say to mine. Curiously enough I happened to be wearing my sword at the time.

"I will not follow you," I replied; "the matter can be settled here?"

"We are observed."

"All the better. Make haste and draw your sword first."

"The advantage is with you."

"I know it, and so it ought to be. If you do not draw I will proclaim you to be the coward I am sure you are."

At this he drew his sword rapidly and came on, but I was ready to receive him. He began to fence to try my mettle, but I lunged right at his chest, and gave him three inches of cold steel. I should have killed him on the spot if he had not lowered his sword, saying he would take his revenge at another time. With this he went off, holding his hand to the wound.

A score of people were close by, but no one troubled himself about the wounded man, as he was known to have been the aggressor. The duel had no further consequences for me. When I left Spa the man was still in the surgeon's hands. He was something worse than an adventurer, and all the French at Spa disowned him.

But to return to Croce and his dinner.

The marchioness, his wife so-called, was a young lady of sixteen or seventeen, fair-complexioned and tall, with all the manners of the Belgian nobility. The history of her escape is well known to her brothers and sisters, and as her family are still in existence my readers will be obliged to me for concealing her name.

Her husband had told her about me, and she received me in the most gracious manner possible. She shewed no signs of sadness or of repentance for the steps she had taken. She was with child for some months, and seemed to be near her term, owing to the slimness of her figure. Nevertheless she had the aspect of perfect health. Her countenance expressed candour and frankness of disposition in a remarkable degree. Her eyes were large and blue, her complexion a roseate hue, her small sweet mouth, her perfect teeth made her a beauty worthy of the brush of Albano.

I thought myself skilled in physiognomy, and concluded that she was not only perfectly happy, but also the cause of happiness. But here let me say how vain a thing it is for anyone to pronounce a man or woman to be happy or unhappy from a merely cursory inspection.

The young marchioness had beautiful ear-rings, and two rings, which gave me a pretext for admiring the beauty of her hands.

Conti's wife did not cut any figure at all, and I was all eyes for the marchioness, whose name was Charlotte. I was profoundly impressed by her that I was quite abstracted during dinner.

I sought in vain to discover by what merits Croce had been able to seduce two such superior women. He was not a fine-looking man, he was not well educated, his manners were doubtful, and his way of speaking by no means seductive; in fine, I saw nothing captivating about him, and yet I could be a witness to his having made two girls leave their homes to follow him. I lost myself in conjecture; but I had no premonition of what was to happen in the course of a few weeks.

When dinner was over I took Croce apart, and talked seriously to him. I impressed on him the necessity of circumspect conduct, as in my opinion he would be for ever infamous if the beautiful woman whom he had seduced was to become wretched by his fault.

"For the future I mean to trust to my skill in play, and thus I am sure of a comfortable living."

"Does she know, that your revenue is fed solely by the purses of dupes?"

"She knows that I am a gamester; and as she adores me, her will is as mine. I am thinking of marrying her at Warsaw before she is confined. If you are in any want of money, look upon my purse as your own."

I thanked him, and once more pressed on him the duty of exercising extreme prudence.

As a matter of fact, I had no need of money. I had played with moderation, and my profits amounted to nearly four hundred louis. When the luck turned against me I was wise enough to turn my back on the board. Although the bruise that Mercy had given me was still apparent, I escorted the marchioness to the tables, and there she drew all eyes upon her. She was fond of piquet, and we played together for small stakes for some time. In the end she lost twenty crowns to me, and I was forced to take the money for fear of offending her.

When we went back we met Croce and Conti, who had both won—Conti a score of louis at Faro, and Croce more than a hundred guineas at 'passe dix', which he had been playing at a club of Englishmen. I was more lively at supper than dinner, and excited Charlotte to laughter by my wit.

Henceforth the Poles and the Tomatis only saw me at intervals. I was in love with the fair marchioness, and everybody said it was very natural. When a week had elapsed, Croce, finding that the pigeons would not come to be plucked, despite the suppers he gave, went to the public room, and lost continually. He was as used to loss as to gain, and his spirits were unaltered; he was still gay, still ate well and drank better, and caressed his victim, who had no suspicions of what was going on.

I loved her, but did not dare to reveal my passion, fearing lest it should be unrequited; and I was afraid to tell her of Croce's losses lest she should put down my action to some ulterior motive; in fine, I was afraid to lose the trust she had already begun to place in me.

At the end of three weeks Conti, who had played with prudence and success, left Croce and set out for Verona with his wife and servant. A few days later Charlotte dismissed her maid, sending her back to Liege, her native town.

Towards the middle of September all the Polish party left the Spa for Paris, where I promised to rejoin them. I only stayed for Charlotte's sake; I foresaw a catastrophe, and I would not abandon her. Every day Croce lost heavily, and at last he was obliged to sell his jewellery. Then came Charlotte's turn; she had to give up her watches, ear-rings, her rings, and all the jewels she had. He lost everything, but this wonderful girl was as affectionate as ever. To make a finish he despoiled her of her lace and her best gowns, and then selling his own wardrobe he went to his last fight with fortune, provided with two hundred Louis. He played like a madman, without common-sense or prudence, and lost all.

His pockets were empty, and seeing me he beckoned to me, and I followed him out of the Spa.

"My friend," he began, "I have two alternatives, I can kill myself this instant or I can fly without returning to the house. I shall embrace the latter and go to Warsaw on foot, and I leave my wife in your hands, for I know you adore her. It must be your task to give her the dreadful news of the pass to which I have come. Have a care of her, she is too good by far for a poor wretch like me. Take her to Paris and I will write to you there at your brother's address. I know you have money, but I would die rather than accept a single Louis from you. I have still two or three pieces left, and I assure you that I am richer at the present moment than I was two months ago. Farewell; once more I commend Charlotte to your care; I would that she had never known me."

With these words he shed tears, and embracing me went his way. I was stupefied at what lay before me.

I had to inform a pregnant woman that the man she dearly loved had deserted her. The only thought that supported me in that moment was that it would be done for love of her, and I felt thankful that I had sufficient means to secure her from privation.

I went to the house and told her that we might dine at once, as the marquis would be engaged till the evening. She sighed, wished him luck, and we proceeded to dine. I disguised my emotions so well that she conceived no suspicion. After the meal was over, I asked her to walk with me in the garden of the Capuchin Monastery, which was close at hand. To prepare her for the fatal news I asked her if she would approve of her lover exposing himself to assassination for the sake of bidding adieu to her rather than making his escape.

"I should blame him for doing so," she replied. "He ought to escape by all means, if only to save his life for my sake. Has my husband done so? Speak openly to me. My spirit is strong enough to resist even so fatal a blow, for I know I have a friend in you. Speak."

"Well, I will tell you all. But first of all remember this; you must look upon me as a tender father who will never let you want, so long as life remains to him."

"In that case I cannot be called unfortunate, for I have a true friend.
Say on."

I told all that Croce had told me, not omitting his last words: "I commend Charlotte to your care; I would that she had never known me."

For a few minutes she remained motionless, as one turned into stone. By her attitude, by her laboured and unequal breath, I could divine somewhat of the battle between love, and anger, and sorrow, and pity, that was raging in the noble breast. I was cut to the heart. At last she wiped away the big tears that began to trickle down her cheeks, and turning to me sighed and said,—

"Dear friend, since I can count on you, I am far indeed from utter misery."

"I swear to you, Charlotte, that I will never leave you till I place you again in your husband's hands, provided I do not die before."

"That is enough. I swear eternal gratitude, and to be as submissive to you as a good daughter ought to be."

The religion and philosophy with which her heart and mind were fortified, though she made no parade of either, began to calm her spirit, and she proceeded to make some reflections on Croce's unhappy lot, but all in pity not in anger, excusing his inveterate passion for play. She had often heard from Croce's lips the story of the Marseilles girl whom he had left penniless in an inn at Milan, commending her to my care. She thought it something wonderful that I should again be intervening as the tutelary genius; but her situation was much the worse, for she was with child.

"There's another difference," I added, "for I made the fortune of the first by finding her an honest husband, whereas I should never have the courage to adopt the same method with the second."

"While Croce lives I am no man's wife but his, nevertheless I am glad to find myself free."

When we were back in the house, I advised her to send away the servant and to pay his journey to Besanion, where she had taken him. Thus all unpleasantness would be avoided. I made her sell all that remained of her poor lover's wardrobe, as also his carriage, for mine was a better one. She shewed me all she had left, which only amounted to some sets of linen and three or four dresses.

We remained at Spa without going out of doors. She could see that my love was a tenderer passion than the love of a father, and she told me so, and that she was obliged to me for the respect with which I treated her. We sat together for hours, she folded in my arms, whilst I gently kissed her beautiful eyes, and asked no more. I was happy in her gratitude and in my powers of self-restraint. When temptation was too strong I left the beautiful girl till I was myself again, and such conquests made me proud. In the affection between us there was somewhat of the purity of a man's first love.

I wanted a small travelling cap, and the servant of the house went to my former lodging to order one. Mercy brought several for me to choose from. She blushed when she saw me, but I said nothing to her. When she had gone I told Charlotte the whole story, and she laughed with all her heart when I reminded her of the bruise on my face when we first met, and informed her that Mercy had given it me. She praised my firmness in rejecting her repentance, and agreed with me in thinking that the whole plan had been concerted between her and her aunt.

We left Spa without any servant, and when we reached Liege we took the way of the Ardennes, as she was afraid of being recognized if we passed through Brussels. At Luxemburg we engaged a servant, who attended on us till we reached Paris. All the way Charlotte was tender and affectionate, but her condition prescribed limits to her love, and I could only look forward to the time after her delivery. We got down at Paris at the "Hotel Montmorenci," in the street of the same name.

Paris struck me quite as a new place. Madame d'Urfe was dead, my friends had changed their houses and their fortunes; the poor had become rich and the rich poor, new streets and buildings were rising on all sides; I hardly knew my way about the town. Everything was dearer; poverty was rampant, and luxury at it highest pitch. Perhaps Paris is the only city where so great a change could take place in the course of five or six years.

The first call I made was on Madame du Rumain, who was delighted to see me. I repaid her the money she had so kindly lent me in the time of my distress. She was well in health, but harassed by so many anxieties and private troubles that she said Providence must have sent me to her to relieve her of all her griefs by my cabala. I told her that I would wait on her at any hour or hours; and this, indeed, was the least I could do for the woman who had been so kind to me.

My brother had gone to live in the Faubourg St. Antoine. Both he and his wife (who remained constant to him, despite his physical disability) were overjoyed to see me, and entreated me to come and stop with them. I told them I should be glad to do so, as soon as the lady who had travelled with me had got over her confinement. I did not think proper to tell them her story, and they had the delicacy to refrain from questioning me on the subject. The same day I called on Princess Lubomirska and Tomatis, begging them not to take it amiss if my visits were few and far between, as the lady they had seen at Spa was approaching her confinement, and demanded all my care.

After the discharge of these duties I remained constantly by Charlotte's side. On October 8th I thought it would be well to take her to Madame Lamarre, a midwife, who lived in the Faubourg St. Denis, and Charlotte was of the same opinion. We went together, she saw the room, the bed, and heard how she would be tended and looked after, for all of which I would pay. At nightfall we drove to the place, with a trunk containing all her effects.

As we were leaving the Rue Montmorenci our carriage was obliged to stop to allow the funeral of some rich man to go by. Charlotte covered her face with her handkerchief, and whispered in my ear, "Dearest, I know it is a foolish superstition, but to a woman in my condition such a meeting is of evil omen."

"What, Charlotte! I thought you were too wise to have such silly fears. A woman in child-bed is not a sick woman, and no woman ever died of giving birth to a child except some other disease intervened."

"Yes, my dear philosopher, it is like a duel; there are two men in perfect health, when all of a sudden there comes a sword-thrust, and one of them is dead."

"That's a witty idea. But bid all gloomy thoughts go by, and after your child is born, and we have placed it in good hands, you shall come with me to Madrid, and there I hope to see you happy and contented."

All the way I did my best to cheer her, for I knew only too well the fatal effects of melancholy on a pregnant woman, especially in such a delicate girl as Charlotte.

When I saw her completely settled I returned to the hotel, and the next day I took up my quarters with my brother. However, as long as my Charlotte lived, I only slept at his house, for from nine in the morning till after midnight I was with my dear.

On October 13th Charlotte was attacked with a fever which never left her. On the 17th she was happily delivered of a boy, which was immediately taken to the church and baptized at the express wishes of the mother. Charlotte wrote down what its name was to be—Jacques (after me), Charles (after her), son of Antonio della Croce and of Charlotte de (she gave her real name). When it was brought from the church she told Madame Lamarre to carry it to the Foundling Hospital, with the certificate of baptism in its linen. I vainly endeavoured to persuade her to leave the care of the child to me. She said that if it lived the father could easily reclaim it. On the same day, October 18th, the midwife gave me the following certificate, which I still possess:

It was worded as follows:

"We, J. B. Dorival, Councillor to the King, Commissary of the Chatelet, formerly Superintendent of Police in the City of Paris, do certify that there has been taken to the Hospital for Children a male infant, appearing to be one day old, brought from the Faubourg St. Denis by the midwife Lamarre, and bearing a certificate of baptism to the effect that its name is Jacques Charles, son of Antonio della Croce and of Charlotte de——. Wherefore, we have delivered the above certificate at our office in the City of Paris, this 18th day of October, in the year of our Lord, 1767, at seven o'clock in the afternoon.

"DORIVAL."

If any of my readers have any curiosity to know the real name of the mother, I have given them the means of satisfying it.

After this I did not leave the bed of the invalid for a single instant. In spite of all the doctor's care the fever increased, and at five o'clock in the morning of October 26th, she succumbed to it. An hour before she sighed her last, she bade me the last farewell in the presence of the venerable ecclesiastic who had confessed her at midnight. The tears which gather fast as I write these words are probably the last honours I shall pay to this poor victim of a man who is still alive, and whose destiny seemed to be to make women unhappy.

I sat weeping by the bed of her I loved so dearly, and in vain Madame Lamarre tried to induce me to come and sit with her. I loved the poor corpse better than all the world outside.

At noon my brother and his wife came to see me; they had not seen me for a week, and were getting anxious. They saw the body lovely in death; they understood my tears, and mingled theirs with mine. At last I asked them to leave me, and I remained all night by Charlotte's bed, resolved not to leave it till her body had been consigned to the grave.

The day before this morning of unhappy memory my brother had given me several letters, but I had not opened any of them. On my return from the funeral I proceeded to do so, and the first one was from M. Dandolo, announcing the death of M. de Bragadin; but I could not weep. For twenty-two years M. de Bragadin had been as a father to me, living poorly, and even going into debt that I might have enough. He could not leave me anything, as his property was entailed, while his furniture and his library would become the prey of his creditors. His two friends, who were my friends also, were poor, and could give me nothing but their love. The dreadful news was accompanied by a bill of exchange for a thousand crowns, which he had sent me twenty-four hours before his death, foreseeing that it would be the last gift he would ever make me.

I was overwhelmed, and thought that Fortune had done her worst to me.

I spent three days in my brother's house without going out. On the fourth I began to pay an assiduous court to Princess Lubomirska, who had written the king, her brother, a letter that must have mortified him, as she proved beyond a doubt that the tales he had listened to against me were mere calumny. But your kings do not allow so small a thing to vex or mortify them. Besides, Stanislas Augustus had just received a dreadful insult from Russia. Repnin's violence in kidnapping the three senators who had spoken their minds at the Diet was a blow which must have pierced the hapless king to the heart.

The princess had left Warsaw more from hatred than love; though such was not the general opinion. As I had decided to visit the Court of Madrid before going to Portugal, the princess gave me a letter of introduction to the powerful Count of Aranda; and the Marquis Caraccioli, who was still at Paris, gave me three letters, one for Prince de la Catolica, the Neapolitan ambassador at

Madrid, one for the Duke of Lossada, the king's favourite and lord high steward, and a third for the Marquis Mora Pignatelli.

On November 4th I went to a concert with a ticket that the princess had given me. When the concert was half-way through I heard my name pronounced, accompanied by scornful laughter. I turned round and saw the gentleman who was speaking contemptuously of me. It was a tall young man sitting between two men advanced in years. I stared him in the face, but he turned his head away and continued his impertinencies, saying, amongst other things, that I had robbed him of a million francs at least by my swindling his late aunt, the Marchioness d'Urfe.

"You are an impudent liar," I said to him, "and if we were out of this room I would give you a kick to teach you to speak respectfully."

With these words I made my way out of the hall, and on turning my head round I saw that the two elderly men were keeping the young blockhead back. I got into my carriage and waited some time, and as he did not come I drove to the theatre and chanced to find myself in the same box as Madame Valville. She informed me that she had left the boards, and was kept by the Marquis the Brunel.

"I congratulate you, and wish you good luck."

"I hope you will come to supper at my house."

"I should be only too happy, but unfortunately I have an engagement; but
I will come and see you if you will give me your address."

So saying, I slipped into her hand a rouleau, it being the fifty Louis I owed her.

"What is this?"

"The money you lent me so kindly at Konigsberg."

"This is neither the time nor the place to return it. I will only take it at my own house, so please do not insist."

I put the money back into my pocket, she gave me her address, and I left her. I felt too sad to visit her alone.

Two days later, as I was at table with my brother, my sister-in-law, and some young Russians whom he was teaching to paint, I was told that a Chevalier of St. Louis wanted to speak to me in the antechamber. I went out, and he handed me a paper without making any preface. I opened the document, and found it was signed "Louis." The great king ordered me to leave Paris in twenty-four hours and his realm of France within three weeks, and the reason assigned was: "It is our good pleasure."

CHAPTER III

My Departure From Paris—My Journey to Madrid—The Count of Aranda—The
Prince de la Catolica—The Duke of Lossada—Mengs—A Ball—Madame
Pichona—Donna Ignazia

"Well, chevalier," I said, "I have read the little note, and I will try and oblige his majesty as soon as possible. However, if I have not time to get away in twenty-four hours, his majesty must work his dread will on me."

"My dear sir, the twenty-four hours are a mere formality. Subscribe the order and give me a receipt for the lettre de cachet, and you can go at your convenience. All I ask of you is that you give me your word of honour not to go to the theatres or public places of amusement on foot."

"I give you my word with pleasure."

I took the chevalier to my room and gave him the necessary acknowledgment, and with the observation that he would be glad to see my brother, whom he knew already, I led him into the dining-room, and explained with a cheerful face the purport of his visit.

My brother laughed and said,—

"But, M. Buhot, this news is like March in Lent, it was quite unnecessary; my brother was going in the course of a week."

"All the better. If the minister had been aware of that he would not have troubled himself about it."

"Is the reason known?"

"I have heard something about a proposal to kick a gentleman, who though young, is too exalted a person to be spoken to in such a manner."

"Why, chevalier," said I, "the phrase is a mere formality like the twenty-four hours for if the impudent young rascal had come out he would have met me, and his sword should have been sufficient to ward off any kicks."

I then told the whole story, and Buhot agreed that I was in the right throughout; adding that the police were also in the right to prevent any encounter between us. He advised me to go next morning and tell the tale to M. de Sartine, who knew me, and would be glad to have the account from my own lips. I said nothing, as I knew the famous superintendent of police to be a dreadful sermoniser.

The lettre de cachet was dated November 6th, and I did not leave Paris till the 20th.

I informed all my friends of the great honour his majesty had done me, and I would not hear of Madame du Rumain appealing to the king on my behalf, though she said she felt certain she could get the order revoked. The Duc de Choiseul gave me a posting passport dated November 19th, which I still preserve.

I left Paris without any servant, still grieving, though quietly, over Charlotte's fate. I had a hundred Louis in cash, and a bill of exchange on Bordeaux for eight thousand francs. I enjoyed perfect health, and almost felt as if I had been rejuvenated. I had need of the utmost prudence and discretion for the future. The deaths of M. de Bragadin and Madame d'Urfe had left me alone in the world, and I was slowly but steadily approaching what is called a certain age, when women begin to look on a man with coldness.

I only called on Madame Valville on the eve of my departure: and found her in a richly-furnished house, and her casket well filled with diamonds. When I proposed to return her the fifty louis, she asked me if I had got a thousand; and on learning that I had only five hundred she refused the money absolutely and offered me her purse, which I in my turn refused. I have not seen the excellent creature since then, but before I left I gave her some excellent advice as to the necessity of saving her gains for the time of her old age, when her charms would be no more. I hope she has profited by my counsel. I bade farewell to my brother and my sister-in-law at six o'clock in the evening, and got into my chaise in the moonlight, intending to travel all night so as to dine next day at Orleans, where I wanted to see an old friend. In half an hour I was at Bourg-la-Reine, and there I began to fall asleep. At seven in the morning I reached Orleans.

Fair and beloved France, that went so well in those days, despite lettres de cachet, despite corvees, despite the people's misery and the king's "good pleasure," dear France, where art thou now? Thy sovereign is the people now, the most brutal and tyrannical sovereign in the world. You have no longer to bear the "good pleasure" of the sovereign, but you have to endure the whims of the mob and the fancies of the Republic—the ruin of all good Government. A republic presupposes self-denial and a virtuous people; it cannot endure long in our selfish and luxurious days.

I went to see Bodin, a dancer, who had married Madame Joffroy, one of my thousand mistresses whom I had loved twenty-two years ago, and had seen later at Turin, Paris, and Vienna. These meetings with old friends and sweethearts were always a weak or rather a strong point with me. For a moment I seemed to be young again, and I fed once more on the delights of long ago. Repentance was no part of my composition.

Bodin and his wife (who was rather ugly than old-looking, and had become pious to suit her husband's tastes, thus giving to God the devil's leavings), Bodin, I say, lived on a small estate he had purchased, and attributed all the agricultural misfortunes he met with in the course of the year to the wrath of an avenging Deity.

I had a fasting dinner with them, for it was Friday, and they strictly observed all the rules of the Church. I told them of my adventures of the past years, and when I had finished they proceeded to make reflections on the faults and failings of men who have not God for a guide. They told me what I knew already: that I had an immortal soul, that there was a God that judgeth righteously, and that it was high time for me to take example by them, and to renounce all the pomps and vanities of the world.

"And turn Capuchin, I suppose?"

"You might do much worse."

"Very good; but I shall wait till my beard grows the necessary length in a single night."

In spite of their silliness, I was not sorry to have spent six hours with these good creatures who seemed sincerely repentant and happy in their way, and after an affectionate embrace I took leave of them and travelled all night. I stopped at Chanteloup to see the monument of the taste and magnificence of the Duc de Choiseul, and spent twenty-four hours there. A gentlemanly and polished individual, who did not know me, and for whom I had no introduction, lodged me in a fine suite of rooms, gave me supper, and would only sit down to table with me after I had used all my powers of persuasion. The next day he treated me in the same way, gave me an excellent dinner, shewed me everything, and behaved as if I were some prince, though he did not even ask my name. His attentions even extended to seeing that none of his servants were at hand when I got into my carriage and drove off. This was to prevent my giving money to any of them.

The castle on which the Duc de Choiseul had spent such immense sums had in reality cost him nothing. It was all owing, but he did not trouble himself about that in the slightest degree, as he was a sworn foe to the principle of meum and tuum. He never paid his creditors, and never disturbed his debtors. He was a generous man; a lover of art and artists, to whom he liked to be of service, and what they did for him he looked upon as a grateful offering. He was intellectual, but a hater of all detail and minute research, being of a naturally indolent and procrastinating disposition. His favourite saying was,

"There's time enough for that."

When I got to Poitiers, I wanted to push on to Vivonne; it was seven o'clock in the evening, and two girls endeavoured to dissuade me from this course.

"It's very cold," said they, "and the road is none of the best. You are no courier, sup here, we will give you a good bed, and you shall start again in the morning."

"I have made up my mind to go on, but if you will keep me company at supper I will stay."

"That would cost you too dearly."

"Never too dear. Quick I make up your minds."

"Well, we will sup with you."

"Then lay the table for three; I must go on in an hour."

"In an hour! You mean three, sir; papa will take two hours to get you a good supper."

"Then I will not go on, but you must keep me company all night."

"We will do so, if papa does not object. We will have your chaise put into the coach-house."

These two minxes gave me an excellent supper, and were a match for me in drinking as well as eating. The wine was delicious, and we stayed at table till midnight, laughing and joking together, though without overstepping the bounds of propriety.

About midnight, the father came in jovially, and asked me how I had enjoyed my supper.

"Very much," I answered, "but I have enjoyed still more the company of your charming daughters."

"I am delighted to hear it. Whenever you come this way they shall keep you company, but now it is past midnight, and time for them to go to bed."

I nodded my head, for Charlotte's death was still too fresh in my memory to admit of my indulging in any voluptuous pleasures. I wished the girls a pleasant sleep, and I do not think I should even have kissed them if the father had not urged me to do this honour to their charms. However, my vanity made me put some fire into the embrace, and I have no doubt they thought me a prey to vain desires.

When I was alone I reflected that if I did not forget Charlotte I was a lost man. I slept till nine o'clock, and I told the servant that came to light my fire to get coffee for three, and to have my horses put in.

The two pretty girls came to breakfast with me, and I thanked them for having made me stay the night. I asked for the bill, and the eldest said it was in round figures a Louis apiece. I shewed no sign of anger at this outrageous fleecing, but gave them three Louis with the best grace imaginable and went on my way. When I reached Angouleme, where I expected to find Noel, the King of Prussia's cook, I only found his father, whose talents in the matter of pates was something prodigious. His eloquence was as fervent as his ovens. He said he would send his pates all over Europe to any address I liked to give him.

"What! To Venice, London, Warsaw, St. Petersburg?"

"To Constantinople, if you like. You need only give me your address, and you need not pay me till you get the pates."

I sent his pates to my friends in Venice, Warsaw, and Turin, and everybody thanked me for the delicious dish.

Noel had made quite a fortune. He assured me he had sent large consignments to America, and with the exception of some losses by shipwreck all the pates had arrived in excellent condition. They were chiefly made of turkeys, partridges, and hare, seasoned with truffles, but he also made pates de foie gras of larks and of thrushes, according to the season.

In two days I arrived at Bordeaux, a beautiful town coming only second to Paris, with respect to Lyons be it said. I spent a week there, eating and drinking of the best, for the living there is the choicest in the world.

I transferred my bill of exchange for eight thousand francs to a Madrid house, and crossed the Landes, passing by Mont de Marsan, Bayonne, and St. Jean de Luz, where I sold my post-chaise. From St. Jean de Luz I went to Pampeluna by way of the Pyrenees, which I crossed on mule-back, my baggage being carried by another mule. The mountains struck me as higher than the Alps. In this I may possibly be wrong, but I am certain that the Pyrenees are the most picturesque, fertile, and agreeable of the two.

At Pampeluna a man named Andrea Capello took charge of me and my luggage, and we set out for Madrid. For the first twenty leagues the travelling was easy enough, and the roads as good as any in France. These roads did honour to the memory of M. de Gages, who had administered Navarre after the Italian war, and had, as I was assured, made the road at his own expense. Twenty years earlier I had been arrested by this famous general; but he had established a claim on posterity greater than any of his victories. These laurels were dyed in blood, but the maker of a good road is a solid benefactor of all posterity.

In time this road came to an end, and thenceforth it would be incorrect to say that the roads were bad, for, to tell the truth, there were no roads at all. There were steep ascents and violent descents, but no traces of carriage wheels, and so it is throughout the whole of Old Castile. There are no good inns, only miserable dens scarce good enough for the muleteers, who make their beds beside their animals. Signor or rather Senor Andrea tried to choose the least wretched inns for me, and after having provided for the mules he would go round the entire village to get something for me to eat. The landlord would not stir; he shewed me a room where I could sleep if I liked, containing a fire-place, in which I could light a fire if I thought fit, but as to procuring firewood or provisions, he left that all to me. Wretched Spain!

The sum asked for a night's accommodation was less than a farmer would ask in France or Germany for leave to sleep in his barn; but there was always an extra charge of a 'pizetta por el ruido'. The pizetta is worth four reals; about twenty-one French sous.

The landlord smoked his paper cigarette nonchalantly enough, blowing clouds of smoke into the air with immense dignity. To him poverty was as good as riches; his wants were small, and his means sufficed for them. In no country in Europe do the lower orders live so contentedly on a very little as in Spain. Two ounces of white bread, a handful of roast chestnuts or acorns (called bellotas in Spanish) suffice to keep a Spaniard for a day. It is his glory to say when a stranger is departing from his abode,—

"I have not given myself any trouble in waiting on him."

This proceeds in part from idleness and in part from Castilian pride. A Castilian should not lower himself, they say, by attending on a Gavacho, by which name the Spaniards know the French, and, indeed, all foreigners. It is not so offensive as the Turkish appellation of dog, or the damned foreigner of the English. Of course, persons who have travelled or have had a liberal education do not speak in this way, and a respectable foreigner will find reasonable Spaniards as he will find reasonable Turks and Englishmen.

On the second night of my journey I slept at Agreda, a small and ugly town, or rather village. There Sister Marie d'Agreda became so crazy as to write a life of the Virgin, which she affirmed to have been dictated to her by the Mother of the Lord. The State

Inquisitors had given me this work to read when I was under the Leads, and it had nearly driven me mad.

We did ten Spanish leagues a day, and long and weary leagues they seemed to me. One morning I thought I saw a dozen Capuchins walking slowly in front of us, but when we caught them up I found they were women of all ages.

"Are they mad?" I said to Senior Andrea.

"Not at all. They wear the Capuchin habit out of devotion, and you would not find a chemise on one of them."

There was nothing surprising in their not having chemises, for the chemise is a scarce article in Spain, but the idea of pleasing God by wearing a Capuchin's habit struck me as extremely odd. I will here relate an amusing adventure which befell me on my way.

At the gate of a town not far from Madrid I was asked for my passport. I handed it over, and got down to amuse myself. I found the chief of the customs' house engaged in an argument with a foreign priest who was on his way to Madrid, and had no passport for the capital. He skewed one he had had for Bilbao, but the official was not satisfied. The priest was a Sicilian, and I asked him why he had exposed himself to being placed in this disagreeable predicament. He said he thought it was unnecessary to have a passport in Spain when one had once journeyed in the country.

"I want to go to Madrid," said he to me, "and hope to obtain a chaplaincy in the house of a grandee. I have a letter for him."

"Shew it; they will let you pass then."

"You are right."

The poor priest drew out the letter and skewed it to the official, who opened it, looked at the signature, and absolutely shrieked when he saw the name Squillace.

"What, senor abbe! you are going to Madrid with a letter from Squillace, and you dare to skew it?"

The clerks, constables, and hangers-on, hearing that the hated Squillace, who would have been stoned to death if it had not been for the king's protection, was the poor abbe's only patron, began to beat him violently, much to the poor Sicilian's astonishment.

I interposed, however, and after some trouble I succeeded in rescuing the priest, who was then allowed to pass, as I believe, as a set-off against the blows he had received.

Squillace was sent to Venice as Spanish ambassador, and in Venice he died at an advanced age. He was a man designed to be an object of intense hatred to the people; he was simply ruthless in his taxation.

The door of my room had a lock on the outside but none on the inside. For the first and second night I let it pass, but on the third I told Senor Andrea that I must have it altered.

"Senor Don Jacob, you must bear with it in Spain, for the Holy Inquisition must always be at liberty to inspect the rooms of foreigners."

"But what in the devil's name does your cursed Inquisition want . . . ?"

"For the love of God, Senor Jacob, speak not thus! if you were overheard we should both be undone."

"Well, what can the Holy Inquisition want to know?"

"Everything. It wants to know whether you eat meat on fast days, whether persons of opposite sexes sleep together, if so, whether they are married, and if not married it will cause both parties to be imprisoned; in fine, Senor Don Jaimo, the Holy inquisition is continually watching over our souls in this country."

When we met a priest bearing the viaticum to some sick man, Senor Andrea would tell me imperatively to get out of my carriage, and then there was no choice but to kneel in the mud or dust as the case might be. The chief subject of dispute at that time was the fashion of wearing breeches. Those who wore 'braguettes' were imprisoned, and all tailors making breeches with 'braguettes' were severely punished. Nevertheless, people persisted in wearing them, and the priests and monks preached in vain against the indecency of such a habit. A revolution seemed imminent, but the matter was happily settled without effusion of blood. An edict was published and affixed to the doors of all the churches, in which it was declared that breeches with braguettes were only to be worn by the public hangmen. Then the fashion passed away; for no one cared to pass for the public executioner.

By little and little I got an insight into the manners of the Spanish nation as I passed through Guadalaxara and Alcala, and at length arrived at Madrid.

Guadalaxara, or Guadalajara, is pronounced by the Spaniards with a strong aspirate, the x and j having the same force. The vowel a, the queen of letters, reigns supreme in Spain; it is a relic of the old Moorish language. Everyone knows that the Arabic abounds in a's, and perhaps the philologists are right in calling it the most ancient of languages, since the a is the most natural and easy to pronounce of all the letters. It seems to me very mistaken to call such words as Achald, Ayanda, Almanda, Acard, Agracaramba, Alcantara, etc., barbarous, for the sonorous ring with which they are pronounced renders the Castilian the richest of all modern languages. Spanish is undoubtedly one of the finest, most energetic, and most majestic languages in the world. When it is pronounced 'ore rotundo' it is susceptible of the most poetic harmony. It would be superior to the Italian, if it were not for the three guttural letters, in spite of what the Spaniards say to the contrary. It is no good remonstrating with them.

'Quisquis amat ranam, ranam purat esse Dianam'.

As I was entering the Gate of Alcala, my luggage was searched, and the clerks paid the greatest attention to my books, and they were very disappointed only to find the "Iliad" in Greek, and a Latin Horace. They were taken away, but three days after, they were returned to me at my lodging in the Rue de la Croix where I had gone in spite of Senor Andrea, who had wanted to take me elsewhere. A worthy man whom I had met in Bordeaux had given me the address. One of the ceremonies I had to undergo at the Gate of Alcala displeased me in the highest degree. A clerk asked me for a pinch of snuff, so I took out my snuff-box and gave it him, but instead of taking a pinch he snatched it out of my hands and said,—

"Senor, this snuff will not pass in Spain" (it was French rappee); and after turning it out on the ground he gave me back the box.

The authorities are most rigorous on the matter of this innocent powder, and in consequence an immense contraband trade is carried on. The spies employed by the Spanish snuff-makers are always on the look-out after foreign snuff, and if they detect anyone carrying it they make him pay dearly for the luxury. The ambassadors of foreign powers are the only persons exempted from the prohibitions. The king who stuffs into his enormous nose one enormous pinch as he rises in the morning wills that all his subjects buy their snuff of the Spanish manufacturers. When Spanish snuff is pure it is very good, but at the time I was in Spain the genuine article could hardly be bought for its weight in gold. By reason of the natural inclination towards forbidden fruit, the Spaniards are extremely fond of foreign snuff, and care little for their own; thus snuff is smuggled to an enormous extent.

My lodging was comfortable enough, but I felt the want of a fire as the cold was more trying than that of Paris, in spite of the southern latitude. The cause of this cold is that Madrid is the highest town in Europe. From whatever part of the coast one starts, one has to mount to reach the capital. The town is also surrounded by mountains and hills, so that the slightest touch of wind from the north makes the cold intense. The air of Madrid is not healthy for strangers, especially for those of a full habit of body; the Spaniards it suits well enough, for they are dry and thin, and wear a cloak even in the dog days.

The men of Spain dwell mentally in a limited horizon, bounded by prejudice on every side; but the women, though ignorant, are usually intelligent; while both sexes are the prey of desires, as lively as their native air, as burning as the sun that shines on them. Every Spaniard hates a foreigner, simply because he is a foreigner, but the women avenge us by loving us, though with great precautions, for your Spaniard is intensely jealous. They watch most jealously over the honour of their wives and daughters. As a rule the men are ugly, though there are numerous exceptions; while the women are pretty, and beauties are not uncommon. The southern blood in their veins inclines them to love, and they are always ready to enter into an intrigue and to deceive the spies by whom they are surrounded. The lover who runs the greatest dangers is always the favourite. In the public walks, the churches, the theatres, the Spanish women are always speaking the language of the eyes. If the person to whom it is addressed knows how to seize the instant, he may be sure of success, but if not, the opportunity will never be offered him again.

I required some kind of heat in my room, and could not bear a charcoal brazier, so I incited an ingenious tin-smith to make me a stove with a pipe going out of the window. However, he was so proud of his success that he made me pay dearly.

Before the stove was ready I was told where I might go and warm myself an hour before noon, and stay till dinner-time. It is called La Pueyta del Sol, "The Gate of the Sun." It is not a gate, but it takes its name from the manner in which the source of all heat lavishes his treasures there, and warms all who come and bask in his rays. I found a numerous company promenading there, walking and talking, but it was not much to my taste.

I wanted a servant who could speak French, and I had the greatest difficulty in getting one, and had to pay dearly, for in Madrid the kind of man I wanted was called a page. I could not compel him to mount behind my carriage, nor to carry a package, nor to light me by night with a torch or lantern.

My page was a man of thirty, and terribly ugly; but this was a recommendation, as his ugliness secured him from the jealous suspicions of husbands. A woman of rank will not drive out without one of these pages seated in the forepart of her carriage. They are said to be more difficult to seduce than the strictest of duennas.

I was obliged to take one of these rascally tribe into my service, and I wish he had broken his leg on his way to my house.

I delivered all my introductions, beginning with the letter from Princess Lubomirska to the Count of Aranda. The count had covered himself with glory by driving the Jesuits out of Spain. He was more powerful than the king himself, and never went out without a number of the royal guardsmen about him, whom he made to sit down at his table. Of course all the Spaniards hated him, but he did not seem to care much for that. A profound politician, and absolutely resolute and firm, he privately indulged in every luxury that he forbade to others, and did not care whether people talked of it or not.

He was a rather ugly man, with a disagreeable squint. His reception of me was far from cordial.

"What do you want in Spain?" he began.

"To add fresh treasures to my store of experience, by observing the manners and the customs of the country, and if possible to serve the Government with such feeble, talents as I may possess."

"Well, you have no need of my protection. If you do not infringe the laws, no one will disturb you. As to your obtaining employment, you had better go to the representative of your country; he will introduce you at Court, and make you known."

"My lord, the Venetian ambassador will do nothing for me; I am in disgrace with the Government. He will not even receive me at the embassy."

"Then I would advise you to give up all hopes of employment, for the king would begin by asking your ambassador about you, and his answer would be fatal. You will do well to be satisfied with amusing yourself."

After this I called on the Neapolitan ambassador, who talked in much the same way. Even the Marquis of Moras, one of the most pleasant men in Spain, did not hold out any hopes. The Duke of Lossada, the high steward and favourite of his Catholic majesty, was sorry to be disabled from doing me any service, in spite of his good will, and advised me, in some way or other, to get the Venetian ambassador to give me a good word, in spite of my disgrace. I determined to follow his advice, and wrote to M. Dandolo, begging him to get the ambassador to favour me at the Spanish Court in spite of my quarrel with the Venetian Government. I worded my letter in such a way that it might be read by the Inquisitors themselves, and calculated on its producing a good impression.

After I had written this letter I went to the lodging of the Venetian ambassador, and presented myself to the secretary, Gaspar Soderini, a worthy and intelligent man. Nevertheless, he dared to tell me that he was astonished at my hardihood in presenting myself at the embassy.

"I have presented myself, sir, that my enemies may never reproach me for not having done so; I am not aware that I have ever done anything which makes me too infamous to call on my ambassador. I should have credited myself with much greater hardihood if I had left without fulfilling this duty; but I shall be sorry if the ambassador views my proceedings in the same light as yourself, and puts down to temerity what was meant for a mark of respect. I shall be none the less astonished if his excellency refuses to receive me on account of a private quarrel between myself and the State Inquisitors, of which he knows no more than I do, and I know nothing. You will excuse my saying that he is not the ambassador of the State Inquisitors, but of the Republic of which I am a subject; for I defy him and I defy the Inquisitors to tell me what crime I have committed that I am to be deprived of my rights as a Venetian citizen. I think that, while it is my duty to reverence my prince in the person of my ambassador, it is his duty to afford me his protection."

This speech had made Soderini blush, and he replied,—

"Why don't you write a letter to the ambassador, with the arguments you have just used to me?"

"I could not write to him before I know whether he will receive me or not. But now, as I have reason to suppose that his opinions are much the same as your own, I will certainly write to him."

"I do not know whether his excellency thinks as I do or not, and, in spite of what I said to you, it is just possible that you do not know my own opinions on the question; but write to him, and he may possibly give you an audience."

"I shall follow your advice, for which I am much obliged."

When I got home I wrote to his excellency all I had said to the secretary, and the next day I had a visit from Count Manucci. The count proved to be a fine-looking young man of an agreeable presence. He said that he lived in the embassy, that his excellency had read my letter, and though he grieved not to receive me publicly he should be delighted to see me in private, for he both knew and esteemed me.

Young Manucci told me that he was a Venetian, and that he knew me by name, as he often heard his father and mother lamenting my fortune. Before long it dawned upon me that this Count Manucci was the son of that Jean Baptiste Manucci who had served as the spy of the State Inquisitors and had so adroitly managed to get possession of my books of magic, which were in all probability the chief corpus delicti.

I did not say anything to him, but I was certain that my guess was correct. His mother was the daughter of a valet de chambre, and his father was a poor mechanic. I asked the young man if he were called count at the embassy, and he said he bore the title in virtue of a warrant from the elector-palatine. My question skewed him that I knew his origin, and he began to speak openly to me; and knowing that I was acquainted with the peculiar tastes of M. de Mocenigo, the ambassador, he informed me laughingly that he was his pathic.

"I will do my best for you," he added; and I was glad to hear him say so, for an Alexis should be able to obtain almost anything from his Corydon. We embraced, and he told me as we parted that he would expect me at the embassy in the afternoon, to take coffee in his room; the ambassador, he said, would certainly come in as soon as he heard of my presence.

I went to the embassy, and had a very kind reception from the ambassador, who said he was deeply grieved not to be able to receive me publicly. He admitted that he might present me at Court without compromising himself, but he was afraid of making enemies.

"I hope soon to receive a letter from a friend of mine, which will authorise your excellency producing me."

"I shall be delighted, in that case, to present you to all the Spanish ministers."

This Mocenigo was the same that acquired such a reputation at Paris by his leanings to pederasty, a vice or taste which the French hold in horror. Later on, Mocenigo was condemned by the Council of Ten to ten years' imprisonment for having started on an embassy to Vienna without formal permission. Maria Theresa had intimated to the Venetian Government that she would not receive such a character, as his habits would be the scandal of her capital. The Venetian Government had some trouble with Mocenigo, and as he attempted to set out for Vienna they exiled him and chose another ambassador, whose morals were as bad, save that the new ambassador indulged himself with Hebe and not Ganymede, which threw a veil of decency over his proceedings.

In spite of his reputation for pederasty, Mocenigo was much liked at Madrid. On one occasion I was at a ball, and a Spaniard noticing me with Manucci, came up to me, and told me with an air of mystery that that young man was the ambassador's wife. He did not know that the ambassador was Manucci's wife; in fact, he did not understand the arrangement at all. "Where ignorance is bliss!" etc. However, in spite of the revolting nature of this vice, it has been a favourite one with several great men. It was well-known to the Ancients, and those who indulged in it were called Hermaphrodites, which symbolises not a man of two sexes but a man with the passions of the two sexes.

I had called two or three times on the painter Mengs, who had been painter in ordinary to his Catholic majesty for six years, and had an excellent salary. He gave me some good dinners. His wife and family were at Rome, while he basked in the royal favours at Madrid, enjoying the unusual privilege of being able to speak to the king whenever he would. At Mengs's house I trade the acquaintance of the architect Sabatini, an extremely able man whom the king had summoned from Naples to cleanse Madrid, which was formerly the dirtiest and most stinking town in Europe, or, for the matter of that, in the world. Sabatini had become a rich man by constructing drains, sewers, and closets for a city of fourteen thousand houses. He had married by proxy the daughter of Vanvitelli, who was also an architect at Naples, but he had never seen her. She came to Madrid about the same time as myself. She was a beauty of eighteen, and no sooner did she see her husband than she declared she would never be his wife. Sabatini was neither a young man nor a handsome one, but he was kind-hearted and distinguished; and when he told his young wife that she would have to choose between him and a nunnery, she determined to make the best of what she thought a bad bargain. However, she had no reason to repent of her choice; her husband was rich, affectionate, and easygoing, and gave her everything she wanted. I sighed and burned for her in silence, not daring to declare my love, for while the wound of the death of Charlotte was still bleeding I also began to find that women were beginning to give me the cold shoulder.

By way of amusing myself I began to go to the theatre, and the masked balls to which the Count of Aranda had established. They

---

were held in a room built for the purpose, and named 'Los Scannos del Peral'. A Spanish play is full of absurdities, but I rather relished the representations. The 'Autos Sacramentales' were still represented; they were afterwards prohibited. I could not help remarking the strange way in which the boxes are constructed by order of the wretched police. Instead of being boarded in front they are perfectly open, being kept up by small pillars. A devotee once said to me at the theatre that this was a very wise regulation, and he was surprised that it was not carried into force in Italy.

"Why so?"

"Because lovers, who feel sure that no one in the pit can see them, may commit improprieties."

I only answered with a shrug of the shoulders.

In a large box opposite to the stage sat 'los padres' of the Holy Inquisition to watch over the morals of actors and audience. I was gazing on them when of a sudden the sentinel at the door of the pit called out "Dios!" and at this cry all the actors and all the audience, men and women, fell down on their knees, and remained kneeling till the sound of a bell in the street ceased to be heard. This bell betokened that a priest was passing by carrying the viaticum to some sick man. I felt very much inclined to laugh, but I had seen enough of Spanish manners to refrain. All the religion of the Spaniard is in outward show and ceremony. A profligate woman before yielding to the desires of her lover covers the picture of Christ, or the Virgin, with a veil. If the lover laughed at this absurdity he would run a risk of being denounced as an

Atheist, and most probably by the wretched woman who had sold him her charms.

In Madrid, and possibly all over Spain, a gentleman who takes a lady to a private room in an inn must expect to have a servant in the room the whole of the time, that he may be able to swear that the couple took no indecent liberties with each other. In spite of all, profligacy is rampant at Madrid, and also the most dreadful hypocrisy, which is more offensive to true piety than open sin. Men and women seemed to have come to an agreement to set the whole system of surveillance utterly at nought. However, commerce with women is not without its dangers; whether it be endemic or a result of dirty habits, one has often good reason to repent the favours one has obtained.

The masked ball quite captivated me. The first time I went to see what it was like and it only cost me a doubloon (about eleven francs), but ever after it cost me four doubloons, for the following reason:

An elderly gentleman, who sat next me at supper, guessed I was a foreigner by my difficulty in making myself understood by the waiter, and asked me where, I had left my lady friend.

"I have not got one; I came by myself to enjoy this delightful and excellently-managed entertainment."

"Yes, but you ought to come with a companion; then you could dance. At present you cannot do so, as every lady has her partner, who will not allow her to dance with anyone else."

"Then I must be content not to dance, for, being a stranger, I do not know any lady whom I can ask to come with me."

"As a stranger you would have much less difficulty in securing a partner than a citizen of Madrid. Under the new fashion, introduced by the Count of Aranda, the masked ball has become the rage of all the women in the capital. You see there are about two hundred of them on the floor to-night; well, I think there are at least four thousand girls in Madrid who are sighing for someone to take them to the ball, for, as you may know, no woman is allowed to come by herself. You would only have to go to any respectable people, give your name and address, and ask to have the pleasure of taking their daughter to the ball. You would have to send her a domino, mask, and gloves; and you would take her and bring her back in your carriage."

"And if the father and mother refused?"

"Then you would make your bow and go, leaving them to repent of their folly, for the girl would sigh, and weep, and moan, bewail parental tyranny, call Heaven to witness the innocency of going to a ball, and finally go into convulsions."

This oration, which was uttered in the most persuasive style, made me quite gay, for I scented an intrigue from afar. I thanked the masked (who spoke Italian very well) and promised to follow his advice and to let him know the results.

"I shall be delighted to hear of your success, and you will find me in the box, where I shall be glad if you will follow me now, to be introduced to the lady who is my constant companion."

I was astonished at so much politeness, and told him my name and followed him. He took me into a box where there were two ladies and an elderly man. They were talking about the ball, so I put in a remark or two on the same topic, which seemed to meet with approval. One of the two ladies, who retained some traces of her former beauty, asked me, in excellent French, what circles I moved in.

"I have only been a short time in Madrid, and not having been presented at Court I really know no one."

"Really! I quite pity you. Come and see me, you will be welcome. My name is Pichona, and anybody will tell you where I live."

"I shall be delighted to pay my respects to you, madam."

What I liked best about the spectacle was a wonderful and fantastic dance which was struck up at midnight. It was the famous fandango, of which I had often heard, but of which I had absolutely no idea. I had seen it danced on the stage in France and Italy, but the actors were careful not to use those voluptuous gestures which make it the most seductive in the world. It cannot be described. Each couple only dances three steps, but the gestures and the attitudes are the most lascivious imaginable. Everything is represented, from the sigh of desire to the final ecstasy; it is a very history of love. I could not conceive a woman refusing her partner anything after this dance, for it seemed made to stir up the senses. I was so excited at this Bacchanalian spectacle that I burst out into cries of delight. The masker who had taken me to his box told me that I should see the fandango danced by the Gitanas with good partners.

"But," I remarked, "does not the Inquisition object to this dance?"

Madame Pichona told me that it was absolutely forbidden, and would not be danced unless the Count of Aranda had given permission.

I heard afterwards that, on the count forbidding the fandango, the ball-room was deserted with bitter complaints, and on the prohibition being withdrawn everyone was loud in his praise.

The next day I told my infamous page to get me a Spaniard who would teach me the fandango. He brought me an actor, who also gave me Spanish lessons, for he pronounced the language admirably. In the course of three days the young actor taught me all the steps so well that, by the confession of the Spaniards themselves, I danced it to perfection.

For the next ball I determined to carry the masker's advice into effect, but I did not want to take a courtesan or a married woman with me, and I could not reasonably expect that any young lady of family would accompany me.

It was St. Anthony's Day, and passing the Church of the Soledad I went in, with the double motive of hearing mass and of procuring a partner for the next day's ball.

I noticed a fine-looking girl coming out of the confessional, with contrite face and lowered eyes, and I noted where she went. She knelt down in the middle of the church, and I was so attracted by her appearance that I registered a mental vow to the effect that she should be my first partner. She did not look like a person of condition, nor, so far as I could see, was she rich, and nothing about her indicated the courtesan, though women of that class go to confession in Madrid like everybody else. When mass was ended, the priest distributed the Eucharist, and I saw her rise and approach humbly to the holy table, and there receive the communion. She then returned to the church to finish her devotions, and I was patient enough to wait till they were over.

At last she left, in company with another girl, and I followed her at a distance. At the end of a street her companion left her to go into her house, and she, retracing her steps, turned into another street and entered a small house, one story high. I noted the house and the street (Calle des Desinjano) and then walked up and down for half an hour, that I might not be suspected of following her. At last I took courage and walked in, and, on my ringing a bell, I heard a voice,

"Who is there?"

"Honest folk," I answered, according to the custom of the country; and the door was opened. I found myself in the presence of a man, a woman, the young devotee I had followed, and another girl, somewhat ugly.

My Spanish was bad, but still it was good enough to express my meaning, and, hat in hand, I informed the father that, being a stranger, and having no partner to take to the ball, I had come to ask him to give me his daughter for my partner, supposing he had a daughter. I assured him that I was a man of honour, and that the girl should be returned to him after the ball in the same condition as when she started.

"Senor," said he, "there is my daughter, but I don't know you, and I don't know whether she wants to go."

"I should like to go, if my parents will allow me."

"Then you know this gentleman?"

"I have never seen him, and I suppose he has never seen me."

"You speak the truth, senora."

The father asked me my name and address, and promised I should have a decisive answer by dinner-time, if I dined at home. I begged him to excuse the liberty I had taken, and to let me know his answer without fail, so that I might have time to get another partner if it were unfavourable to me.

Just as I was beginning to dine my man appeared. I asked him to sit down, and he informed me that his daughter would accept my offer, but that her mother would accompany her and sleep in the carriage. I said that she might do so if she liked, but I should be sorry for her on account of the cold. "She shall have a good cloak," said he; and he proceeded to inform me that he was a cordwainer.

"Then I hope you will take my measure for a pair of shoes."

"I daren't do that; I'm an hidalgo, and if I were to take anyone's measure I should have to touch his foot, and that would be a degradation. I am a cobbler, and that is not inconsistent with my nobility."

"Then, will you mend me these boots?"

"I will make them like new; but I see they want a lot of work; it will cost you a pezzo duro, about five francs."

I told him that I thought his terms very reasonable, and he went out with a profound bow, refusing absolutely to dine with me.

Here was a cobbler who despised bootmakers because they had to touch the foot, and they, no doubt, despised him because he touched old leather. Unhappy pride how many forms it assumes, and who is without his own peculiar form of it?

The next day I sent to the gentleman-cobbler's a tradesman with dominos, masks, and gloves; but I took care not to go myself nor to send my page, for whom I had an aversion which almost amounted to a presentiment. I hired a carriage to seat four, and at nightfall I drove to the house of my pious partner, who was quite ready for me. The happy flush on her face was a sufficient index to me of the feelings of her heart. We got into the carriage with the mother, who was wrapped up in a vast cloak, and at the door of the dancing-room we descended, leaving the mother in the carriage. As soon as we were alone my fair partner told me that her name was Donna Ignazia.

CHAPTER IV

My Amours With Donna Ignazia—My Imprisonment At Buen Retiro—My
Triumph—I Am Commended to the Venetian Ambassador by One of the State
Inquisitors

We entered the ball-room and walked round several times. Donna Ignazia was in such a state of ecstasy that I felt her trembling, and augured well for my amorous projects. Though liberty, nay, license, seemed to reign supreme, there was a guard of soldiers ready to arrest the first person who created any disturbance. We danced several minuets and square dances, and at ten o'clock we went into the supper-room, our conversation being very limited all the while, she not speaking for fear of encouraging me too much, and I on account of my poor knowledge of the Spanish language. I left her alone for a moment after supper, and went to the box, where I expected to find Madame Pichona, but it was occupied by maskers, who were unknown to me, so I rejoined my partner, and we went on dancing the minuets and quadrilles till the fandango was announced. I took my place with my partner, who danced it admirably, and seemed astonished to find herself so well supported by a foreigner. This dance had excited both of us, so, after taking her to the buffet and giving her the best wines and liqueurs procurable, I asked her if she were content with me. I added that I was so deeply in love with her that unless she found some means of making me happy I should undoubtedly die of love. I assured her that I was ready to face all hazards.

"By making you happy," she replied, "I shall make myself happy, too. I will write to you to-morrow, and you will find the letter sewn into the hood of my domino."

"You will find me ready to do anything, fair Ignazia, if you will give me hope."

At last the ball was over, and we went out and got into the carriage. The mother woke up, and the coachman drove off, and I, taking the girl's hands, would have kissed them. However, she seemed to suspect that I had other intentions, and held my hands clasped so tightly that I believe I should have found it a hard task to pull them away. In this position Donna Ignazia proceeded to tell her mother all about the ball, and the delight it had given her. She did not let go my hands till we got to the corner of their street, when the mother called out to the coachman to stop, not wishing to give her neighbours occasion for slander by stopping in front of their own house.

The next day I sent for the domino, and in it I found a letter from Donna Ignazia, in which she told me that a Don Francisco de Ramos would call on me, that he was her lover, and that he would inform me how to render her and myself happy.

Don Francisco wasted no time, for the next morning at eight o'clock my page sent in his name. He told me that Donna Ignazia, with whom he spoke every night, she being at her window and he in the street, had informed him that she and I had been at the ball together. She had also told him that she felt sure I had conceived a fatherly affection for her, and she had consequently prevailed upon him to call on me, being certain that I would treat him as my own son. She had encouraged him to ask me to lend him a hundred doubloons which would enable them to get married before the end of the carnival.

"I am employed at the Mint," he added, "but my present salary is a very small one. I hope I shall get an increase before long, and then I shall be in a position to make Ignazia happy. All my relations live at Toledo, and I have no friends at Madrid, so when we set up our only friends will be the father and mother of my wife and yourself, for I am sure you love her like a daughter."

"You have probed my heart to its core," I replied, "but just now I am awaiting remittances, and have very little money about me. You may count on my discretion, and I shall be delighted to see you whenever you care to call on me."

The gallant made me a bow, and took his departure in no good humour. Don Francisco was a young man of twenty-two, ugly and ill-made. I resolved to nip the intrigue in the bud, for my inclination for Donna Ignazia was of the lightest description; and I went to call on Madame Pichona, who had given me such a polite invitation to come and see her. I had made enquiries about her, and had found out that she was an actress and had been made rich by the Duke of Medina-Celi. The duke had paid her a visit in very cold weather, and finding her without a fire, as she was too poor to buy coals, had sent her the next day a silver stove, which he had filled with a hundred thousand pezzos duros in gold, amounting to three hundred thousand francs in French money.

Since then Madame Pichona lived at her ease and received good company.

She gave me a warm reception when I called on her, but her looks were sad. I began by saying that as I had not found her in her box on the last ball night I had ventured to come to enquire after her health.

"I did not go," said she, "for on that day died my only friend the Duke of Medina-Celi. He was ill for three days."

"I sympathise with you. Was the duke an old man?"

"Hardly sixty. You have seen him; he did not look his age."

"Where have I seen him?"

"Did he not bring you to my box?"

"You don't say so! He did not tell me his name and I never saw him before."

I was grieved to hear of his death; it was in all probability a misfortune for me as well as Madame Pichona. All the duke's estate passed to a son of miserly disposition, who in his turn had a son who was beginning to evince the utmost extravagance.

I was told that the family of Medina-Celi enjoys thirty titles of nobility.

One day a young man called on me to offer me, as a foreigner, his services in a country which he knew thoroughly.

"I am Count Marazzini de Plaisance," he began, "I am not rich and I have come to Madrid to try and make my fortune. I hope to enter the bodyguard of his Catholic majesty. I have been indulging in the amusements of the town ever since I came. I saw you at the ball with an unknown beauty. I don't ask you to tell me her name, but if you are fond of novelty I can introduce you to all the handsomest girls in Madrid."

If my experience had taught me such wholesome lessons as I might have expected, I should have shown the impudent rascal the door. Alas! I began to be weary of my experience and the fruits of it; I began to feel the horrors of a great void; I had need of some slight passion to wile away the dreary hours. I therefore made this Mercury welcome, and told him I should be obliged by his presenting me to some beauties, neither too easy nor too difficult to access.

"Come with me to the ball," he rejoined, "and I will shew you some women worthy of your attention."

The ball was to take place the same evening, and I agreed; he asked me to give him some dinner, and I agreed to that also. After dinner he told me he had no money, and I was foolish enough to give him a doubloon. The fellow, who was ugly, blind of one eye, and full of impudence, shewed me a score of pretty women, whose histories he told me, and seeing me to be interested in one of them he promised to bring her to a procuress. He kept his word, but he cost me dear; for the girl only served for an evening's amusement.

Towards the end of the carnival the noble Don Diego, the father of Donna Ignazia, brought me my boots, and the thanks of his wife and himself for the pleasure I had given her at the ball.

"She is as good as she is beautiful," said I, "she deserves to prosper, and if I have not called on her it is only that I am anxious to do nothing which could injure her reputation."

"Her reputation, Senor Caballero, is above all reproach, and I shall be delighted to see you whenever you honour me with a call."

"The carnival draws near to its end," I replied, "and if Donna Ignazia would like to go to another ball I shall be happy to take her again."

"You must come and ask her yourself."

"I will not fail to do so."

I was anxious to see how the pious girl, who had tried to make me pay a hundred doubloons for the chance of having her after her marriage, would greet me, so I called the same day. I found her with her mother, rosary in hand, while her noble father was botching old boots. I laughed inwardly at being obliged to give the title of don to a cobbler who would not make boots because he was an hidalgo. Hidalgo, meaning noble, is derived from 'higo de albo', son of somebody, and the people, whom the nobles call 'higos de nade', sons of nobody, often revenge themselves by calling the nobles hideputas, that is to say, sons of harlots.

Donna Ignazia rose politely from the floor, where she was sitting cross-legged, after the Moorish fashion. I have seen exalted ladies in this position at Madrid, and it is very common in the antechambers of the Court and the palace of the Princess of the Asturias. The Spanish women sit in church in the same way, and the rapidity with which they can change this posture to a kneeling or a standing one is something amazing.

Donna Ignazia thanked me for honouring her with a visit, adding that she would never have gone to the ball if it had not been for me, and that she never hoped to go to it again, as I had doubtless found someone else more worthy of my attentions.

"I have not found anyone worthy to be preferred before you," I replied, "and if you would like to go to the ball again I should be most happy to take you."

The father and mother were delighted with the pleasure I was about to give to their beloved daughter. As the ball was to take place the same evening, I gave the mother a doubloon to get a mask and domino. She went on her errand, and, as Don Diego also went out on some business, I found myself alone with the girl. I took the opportunity of telling her that if she willed I would be hers, as I adored her, but that I could not sigh for long.

"What can you ask, and what can I offer, since I must keep myself pure for my husband?"

"You should abandon yourself to me without reserve, and you may be sure that I should respect your innocence."

I then proceeded to deliver a gentle attack, which she repulsed, with a serious face. I stopped directly, telling her that she would find me polite and respectful, but not in the least affectionate, for the rest of the evening.

Her face had blushed a vivid scarlet, and she replied that her sense of duty obliged her to repulse me in spite of herself.

I liked this metaphysical line of argument. I saw that I had only to destroy the idea of duty in her and all the rest would follow. What I had to do was to enter into an argument, and to bear away the prize directly I saw her at a loss for an answer.

"If your duty," I began, "forces you to repulse me in spite of yourself, your duty is a burden on you. If it is a burden on you, it is your enemy, and if it is your enemy why do you suffer it thus lightly to gain the victory? If you were your own friend, you would at once expel this insolent enemy from your coasts."

"That may not be."

"Yes, it may. Only shut your eyes."

"Like that?"

"Yes."

I immediately laid hands on a tender place; she repulsed me, but more gently and not so seriously as before.

"You may, of course, seduce me," she said, "but if you really love me you will spare me the shame."

"Dearest Ignazia, there is no shame in a girl giving herself up to the man she loves. Love justifies all things. If you do not love me I ask nothing of you."

"But how shall I convince you that I am actuated by love and not by complaisance?"

"Leave me to do what I like, and my self-esteem will help me to believe you."

"But as I cannot be certain that you will believe me, my duty plainly points to a refusal."

"Very good, but you will make me sad and cold."

"Then I shall be sad, too."

At these encouraging words I embraced her, and obtained some solid favours with one hardy hand. She made no opposition, and I was well pleased with what I had got; and for a first attempt I could not well expect more.

At this juncture the mother came in with the dominos and gloves. I refused to accept the change, and went away to return in my carriage, as before.

Thus the first step had been taken, and Donna Ignazia felt it would be ridiculous not to join in with my conversation at the ball which all tended to procuring the pleasure of spending our nights together. She found me affectionate all the evening, and at supper I did my best to get her everything she liked. I made her see that the part she had at last taken was worthy of praise, and not blame.

I filled her pockets with sweets, and put into my own pockets two bottles of ratafia, which I handed over to the mother, who was asleep in the carriage. Donna Ignazia gratefully refused the quadruple I wished to give her, saying that if it were in my power to make such presents, I might give the money to her lover whenever he called on me.

"Certainly," I answered, "but what shall I say to prevent his taking offence?"

"Tell him that it is on account of what he asked you. He is poor, and I am sure he is in despair at not seeing me in the window to-night. I shall tell him I only went to the ball with you to please my father."

Donna Ignazia, a mixture of voluptuousness and piety, like most Spanish women, danced the fandango with so much fire that no words could have expressed so well the joys that were in store for me. What a dance it is! Her bosom was heaving and her blood all aflame, and yet I was told that for the greater part of the company the dance was wholly innocent, and devoid of any intention. I pretended to believe it, but I certainly did not. Ignazia begged me to come to mass at the Church of the Soledad the next day at eight o'clock. I had not yet told her that it was there I had seen her first. She also asked me to come and see her in the evening, and said she would send me a letter if we were not left alone together.

I slept till noon, and was awoke by Marazzini, who came to ask me to give him some dinner. He told me he had seen me with my fair companion the night before, and that he had vainly

---

endeavoured to find out who she was. I bore with this singularly misplaced curiosity, but when it came to his saying that he would have followed us if he had had any money, I spoke to him in a manner that made him turn pale. He begged pardon, and promised to bridle his curiosity for the future. He proposed a party of pleasure with the famous courtezan Spiletta, whose favours were dear, but I declined, for my mind was taken up with the fair Ignazia, whom I considered a worthy successor to Charlotte.

I went to the church, and she saw me when she came in, followed by the same companion as before.

She knelt down at two or three paces from me, but did not once look in my direction. Her friend, on the other hand, inspected me closely; she seemed about the same age as Ignazia, but she was ugly. I also noticed Don Francisco, and as I was going out of the church my rival followed me, and congratulated me somewhat bitterly on my good fortune in having taken his mistress a second time to the ball. He confessed that he had been on our track the whole evening, and that he should have gone away well enough pleased if it had not been for the way in which we dance the fandango. I felt this was an occasion for a little gentle management, and I answered good-humouredly that the love he thought he noticed was wholly imaginary, and that he was wrong to entertain any suspicions as to so virtuous a girl as Donna Ignazia. At the same time I placed an ounce in his hand, begging him to take it on account. He did so with an astonished stare, and, calling me his father and guardian angel, swore an eternal gratitude.

In the evening I called on Don Diego, where I was regaled with the excellent ratafia I had given the mother, and the whole family began to speak of the obligations Spain owed to the Count of Aranda.

"No exercise is more healthful than dancing," said Antonia, the mother, "and before his time balls were strictly forbidden. In spite of that he is hated for having expelled 'los padres de la compagnia de Jesus', and for his sumptuary regulations. But the poor bless his name, for all the money produced by the balls goes to them."

"And thus," said the father, "to go to the ball is to do a pious work."

"I have two cousins," said Ignazia, "who are perfect angels of goodness. I told them that you had taken me to the ball; but they are so poor that they have no hope of going. If you like you can make them quite happy by taking them on the last day of the carnival. The ball closes at midnight, so as not to profane Ash Wednesday."

"I shall be happy to oblige you, all the more as your lady mother will not be obliged to wait for us in the carriage."

"You are very kind; but I shall have to introduce you to my aunt; she is so particular. When she knows you, I am sure she will consent, for you have all the air of discretion. Go and see her to-day; she lives in the next street, and over her door you will see a notice that lace is washed within. Tell her that my mother gave you the address. To-morrow morning, after mass, I will see to everything else, and you must come here at noon to agree as to our meeting on the last day of the carnival."

I did all this, and the next day I heard that it was settled.

"I will have the dominos ready at my house," I said, "and you must come in at the back door. We will dine in my room, mask, and go to the ball. The eldest of your cousins must be disguised as a man."

"I won't tell her anything about that, for fear she might think it a sin, but once in your house you will have no difficulty in managing her."

The younger of the two cousins was ugly, but looked like a woman, where as the elder looked like an ugly dressed man in woman's clothes. She made an amusing contrast with Donna Ignazia, who looked most seductive when she laid aside her air of piety.

I took care that everything requisite for our disguises should be at hand in a neighbouring closet, unbeknown to my rascally page. I gave him a piece of money in the morning, and told him to spend the last day of the carnival according to his own taste, as I should not require his services till noon the day after.

I ordered a good dinner, and a waiter to serve it, at the tavern, and got rid of Marazzini by giving him a doubloon. I took great pains over the entertainment I was to give the two cousins and the fair Ignazia, whom I hoped that day to make my mistress. It was all quite a novelty for me; I had to do with three devotees, two hideous and the third ravishingly beautiful, who had already had a foretaste of the joys in store for her.

They came at noon, and for an hour I discoursed to them in a moral and unctuous manner. I had taken care to provide myself with some excellent wine, which did not fail to take effect on the three girls, who were not accustomed to a dinner that lasted two hours. They were not exactly inebriated, but their spirits were worked up to a pitch they had never attained before.

I told the elder cousin, who might be twenty-five years old, that I was going to disguise her as a man; consternation appeared on her features, but I had expected as much, and Donna Ignazia told her she was only too lucky, and her sister observed that she did not think it could be a sin.

"If it were a sin," said I, "do you suppose that I should have suggested it to your virtuous sister."

Donna Ignazia, who knew the Legendarium by heart, corroborated my assertion by saying that the blessed St. Marina had passed her whole life in man's clothes; and this settled the matter.

I then burst into a very high-flown eulogium of her intellectual capacity, so as to enlist her vanity in the good cause.

"Come with me," said I, "and do you ladies wait here; I want to enjoy your surprise when you see her in man's clothes."

The ugly cousin made a supreme effort and followed me, and when she had duly inspected her disguise I told her to take off her boots and to put on white stockings and shoes, of which I had provided several pairs. I sat down before her, and told her that if she suspected me of any dishonourable intentions she would commit a mortal sin, as I was old enough to be her father. She replied that she was a good Christian, but not a fool. I fastened her garters for her, saying that I should never have supposed she had so well-shapen and so white a leg, which compliment made her smile in a satisfied manner.

Although I had a fine view of her thighs, I observed no traces of a blush on her face. I then gave her a pair, of my breeches, which fitted her admirably, though I was five inches taller than she, but this difference was compensated by the posterior proportions, with which, like most women, she was bountifully endowed. I turned away to let her put them on in freedom, and, having given her a linen shirt, she told me she had finished before she had buttoned it at the neck. There may possibly have been a little coquetry in this, as I buttoned the shirt for her, and was thus gratified with a sight of her splendid breast. I need not say whether she was pleased or not at my refraining from complimenting her upon her fine proportions. When her toilette was finished I surveyed her from head to foot, and pronounced her to be a perfect man, with the exception of one blemish.

"I am sorry for that."

"Will you allow me to arrange your shirt so as to obviate it?"

"I shall be much obliged, as I have never dressed in man's clothes before."

I then sat down in front of her, and, after unbuttoning the fly, arranged the shirt in a proper manner. In doing so I allowed myself some small liberties, but I toyed with such a serious air that she seemed to take it all as a matter of course.

When I had put on her domino and mask I led her forth, and her sister and Donna Ignazia congratulated her on her disguise, saying that anybody would take her for a man.

"Now it's your turn," I said to the younger one.

"Go with him," said the elder, "Don Jaime is as honest a man as you will find in Spain."

There was really not much to be done to the younger sister, her disguise being simply a mask and domino, but as I wanted to keep Ignazia a long time I made her put on white stockings, change her kerchief, and a dozen other trifles. When she was ready I brought her forth, and Donna Ignazia noticing that she had changed her stockings and kerchief, asked her whether I were as expert at dressing a lady as at turning a lady into a gentleman.

"I don't know," she replied, "I did everything for myself."

Next came the turn of Don Diego's daughter, and as soon as I had her in the closet I did my pleasure on her, she submitting with an air that seemed to say, "I only give in because I can't resist." Wishing to save her honour I withdrew in time, but in the second combat I held her for half an hour to my arms. However, she was naturally of a passionate disposition, and nature had endowed her with a temperament able to resist the most vigorous attacks. When decency made us leave the closet, she remarked to her cousins,

"I thought I should never have done; I had to alter the whole fit of the domino."

I admired her presence of mind.

At nightfall we went to the ball, at which the fandango might be danced ad libitum by a special privilege, but the crowd was so great that dancing was out of the question. At ten we had supper, and then walked up and down, till all at once the two orchestras became silent. We heard the church clocks striking midnight the carnival was over, and Lent had begun.

This rapid transition from wantonness to devotion, from paganism to Christianity, has something startling and unnatural about it. At fifty-nine minutes past eleven the senses are all aglow; midnight sounds, and in a minute they are supposed to be brought low, and the heart to be full of humble repentance; it is an absurdity, an impossibility.

I took the three girls to my house to take off their dominos, and we then escorted the two cousins home. When we had left them for a few minutes Donna Ignazia told me that she would like a little coffee. I understood her, and took her to my house, feeling sure of two hours of mutual pleasure.

I took her to my room, and was just going out to order the coffee when I met Don Francisco, who asked me plainly to let him come up, as he had seen Donna Ignazia go in with me. I had sufficient strength of mind to conceal my rage and disappointment, and told him to come in, adding that his mistress would be delighted at this unexpected visit. I went upstairs, and he followed me, and I shewed him into the room, congratulating the lady on the pleasant surprise.

I expected that she would play her part as well as I had played mine, but I was wrong. In her rage she told him that she would never have asked me to give her a cup of coffee if she had foreseen this piece of importunity, adding that if he had been a gentleman he would have known better than to intrude himself at such an hour.

In spite of my own anger I felt that I must take the poor devil's part; he looked like a dog with a tin kettle tied to his tail. I tried to calm Donna Ignazia, telling her that Don Francisco had seen us by a mere accident, and that it was I who had asked him to come upstairs, in the hope of pleasing her.

Donna Ignazia feigned to be persuaded and asked her lover to sit down, but she did not speak another word to him, confining her remarks to me, saying how much she had enjoyed the ball, and how kind I had been to take her cousins.

After he had taken a cup of coffee, Don Francisco bade us a good night. I told him I hoped he would come and see me before Lent was over, but Donna Ignazia only vouchsafed him a slight nod. When he had gone she said, sadly enough, that she was sorry he had deprived us both of our pleasure, and that she was sure Don Francisco was still hanging about the place, and that she dared not expose herself to his vengeance. "So take me home, but if you love me come and see me again. The trick the stupid fellow has played me shall cost him dear. Are you sure I don't love him?"

"Quite certain, for you love me too well to love anybody else."

Donna Ignazia gave me a hasty proof of her affection, and I escorted her home, assuring her that she would be the sole object of my thoughts as long as I stayed at Madrid.

The next day I dined with Mengs, and the day after that I was accosted in the street by an ill-looking fellow, who bade me follow him to a cloister, as he had something of importance to communicate to me.

As soon as he saw that we were unobserved, he told me that the Alcalde Messa was going to pay me a visit that same night with a band of police, "of whom," he added, "I am one. He knows you have concealed weapons in your room. He knows, or thinks he knows, certain other things which authorize him to seize your person and to take you to the prison where persons destined for the galleys are kept. I give you all this warning because I believe you to be a man of honour. Despise not my advice, but look to yourself, and get into some place of security."

I credited what he told me, as the circumstance of my having arms was perfectly true, so I gave the man a doubloon, and, instead of calling on Donna Ignazia, as I intended, I went back to my lodging, and after putting the weapons under my cloak I went to Mengs's, leaving word at the cafe to send me my page as soon as he came back. In Mengs's house I was safe, as it belonged to the king.

The painter was an honest fellow, but proud and suspicious in excess. He did not refuse me an asylum for the night, but he told me that I must look out for some other refuge, as the alcalde must have some other accusation against me, and that knowing nothing of the merits or demerits of the case he could not take any part in it. He gave me a room and we supped together, discussing the matter all the time, I persisting that the possession of arms was my only offence, and he replying that if it were so I should have awaited the alcalde fearlessly, as it stood to reason that a man had a right to keep defensive weapons in his own room. To this I answered that I had only come to him to avoid passing the night in prison, as I was certain that the man had told me the truth.

"To-morrow I shall look out for another lodging."

I confessed, however, that it would have been wiser of me to leave my pistols and musket in my room.

"Yes, and you might have remained there yourself. I did not think you were so easily frightened."

As we were arguing it over my landlord came and said that the alcalde with thirty constables had been to my apartment and had broken open the door. He had searched everything, but unsuccessfully, and had gone away after sealing the room and its contents. He had arrested and imprisoned my page on the charge of having warned me, "for otherwise," he said, "the Venetian gentleman would never have gone to the house of Chevalier Mengs, where he is out of my power."

At this Mengs agreed that I had been right in believing my informant's tale, and he added that the first thing in the morning I should go and protest my innocence before the Count of

Aranda, but he especially urged on me the duty of defending the poor page. My landlord went his way, and we continued the discussion, Mengs insisting on the page's innocence, till at last I lost all patience, and said,—

"My page must be a thorough-paced scoundrel; the magistrate's arresting him for warning me is an absolute proof that he knew of my approaching arrest. What is a servant who does not warn his master under such circumstances but a rascal? Indeed I am absolutely certain that he was the informer, for he was the only person who knew where the arms were concealed."

Mengs could find no answer to this, and left to go to bed. I did the same and had an excellent night.

Early the next morning the great Mengs sent me linen and all the requisites of the toilette. His maid brought me a cup of chocolate, and his cook came to ask if I had permission to eat flesh-meat. In such ways a prince welcomes a guest, and bids him stay, but such behaviour in a private person is equivalent to a hint to go. I expressed my gratitude, and only accepted a cup of chocolate and one handkerchief.

My carriage was at the door, and I was just taking leave of Mengs when an officer appeared on the scene, and asked the painter if the Chevalier de Casanova was in his house.

"I am the Chevalier de Casanova," said I.

"Then I hope you will follow me of your own free will to the prison of Buen Retiro. I cannot use force here, for this house is the king's, but I warn you that in less than an hour the Chevalier Mengs will have orders to turn you out, and then you will be dragged to prison, which would be unpleasant for you. I therefore advise you to follow me quietly, and to give up such weapons as you may possess."

"The Chevalier Mengs will give you the weapons in question. I have carried them with me for eleven years; they are meant to protect me on the highways. I am ready to follow you, but first allow me to write four notes; I shall not be half an hour."

"I can neither allow you to wait nor to write, but you will be at liberty to do so after you have reached the prison."

"Very good; then I am ready to follow you, for I have no choice. I shall remember Spanish justice!"

I embraced Mengs, had the weapons put into my carriage, and got in with the officer, who seemed a perfect gentleman.

He took me to the Castle of Buen Retiro, formerly a royal palace, and now a prison. When my conductor had consigned me to the officer of the watch I was handed over to a corporal, who led me into a vast hall on the ground floor of the building. The stench was dreadful, and the prisoners were about thirty, ten of them being soldiers. There were ten or twelve large beds, some benches, no tables, and no chairs.

I asked a guard to get me some pens, ink, and paper, and gave him a duro for the purpose. He took the coin smilingly, and went away, but he did not return. When I asked his brethren what had become of him they laughed in my face. But what surprised me the most was the sight of my page and Marazzini, who told me in Italian that he had been there for three days, and that he had not written to me as he had a presentiment that we should soon meet. He added that in a fortnight's time we should be sent off under a heavy escort to work in some fortress, though we might send our pleas to the Government, and might possibly be let out after three or four years' imprisonment.

"I hope," he said, "not to be condemned before I am heard. The alcalde will come and interrogate you tomorrow, and your answers will be taken down; that's all. You may then be sent to hard labour in Africa."

"Has your case been heard yet?"

"They were at me about it for three hours yesterday."

"What kind of questions did they ask you?"

"They wished to know what banker furnished me with money for my expenses. I told them I had not got a banker, and that I lived by borrowing from my friends, in the expectation of becoming one of the king's body-guard. They then asked me how it was that the Parmese ambassador knew nothing about me, and I replied that I had never been presented to him.

"'Without the favour of your ambassador,' they objected, 'you could never join the royal guard, and you must be aware of that, but the king's majesty shall give you employment where you will stand in need of no commendation;' and so the alcalde left me. If the Venetian ambassador does not interpose in your behalf you will be treated in the same way."

I concealed my rage, and sat down on a bed, which I left after three hours, as I found myself covered with the disgusting vermin which seem endemic in Spain. The very sight of them made me sick. I stood upright, motionless, and silent, devouring the bile which consumed me.

There was no good in talking; I must write; but where was I to find writing materials? However, I resolved to wait in silence; my time must come, sooner or later.

At noon Marazzini told me that he knew a soldier for whose trustworthiness he would answer, and who would get me my dinner if I gave him the money.

"I have no appetite," I replied, "and I am not going to give a farthing to anyone till the stolen crown is restored to me."

He made an uproar over this piece of cheating, but the soldiers only laughed at him. My page then asked him to intercede with me, as he was hungry, and had no money wherewith to buy food.

"I will not give him a farthing; he is no longer in my service, and would to God I had never seen him!"

My companions in misery proceeded to dine on bad garlic soup and wretched bread, washed down by plain water, two priests and an individual who was styled corregidor excepted, and they seemed to fare very well.

At four o'clock one of Mengs's servants brought me a dinner which would have sufficed for four. He wanted to leave me the dinner and come for the plates in the evening; but not caring to share the meal with the vile mob around me I made him wait till I had done and come again at the same time the next day, as I did not require any supper. The servant obeyed. Marazzini said rudely that I might at least have kept the bottle of wine; but I gave him no answer.

At five o'clock Manucci appeared, accompanied by a Spanish officer. After the usual compliments had passed between us I asked the officer if I might write to my friends, who would not allow me to stay much longer in prison if they were advised of my arrest.

"We are no tyrants," he replied; "you can write what letters you like."

"Then," said I, "as this is a free country, is it allowable for a soldier who has received certain moneys to buy certain articles to pocket the money and appropriate it to his own use?"

"What is his name?"

The guard had been relieved, and no one seemed to know who or where he was.

"I promise you, sir," said the officer, "that the soldier shall be punished and your money restored to you; and in the meanwhile you shall have pens, ink, paper, a table, and a candle, immediately."

"And I," added Manucci, "promise you that one of the ambassador's servants shall wait on you at eight o'clock to deliver any letters you may write."

I took three crowns from my pocket, and told my fellow-prisoners that the first to name the soldier who had deceived me should have the money; Marazzini was the first to do so. The officer made a note of the man's name with a smile; he was beginning to know me; I had spent three crowns to get back one, and could not be very avaricious.

Manucci whispered to me that the ambassador would do his best in a confidential way to get my release, and that he had no doubt of his success.

When my visitors were gone I sat down to write, but I had need of all my patience. The rascally prisoners crowded round me to read what I was writing, and when they could not understand it they were impudent enough to ask me to explain it to them. Under the pretext of snuffing the candle, they put it out. However, I bore with it all. One of the soldiers said he would keep them quiet for a crown, but I gave him no answer. In spite of the hell around me, I finished my letters and sealed them up. They were no studied or rhetorical epistles, but merely the expression of the fury with which I was consumed.

I told Mocenigo that it was his duty to defend a subject of his prince, who had been arrested and imprisoned by a foreign power on an idle pretext. I shewed him that he must give me his protection unless I was guilty, and that I had committed no offence against the law of the land. I reminded him that I was a Venetian, in spite of my persecution at the hands of the State Inquisitors, and that being a Venetian I had a right to count on his protection.

To Don Emmanuel de Roda, a learned scholar, and the minister of justice,
I wrote that I did not ask any favour but only simple justice.

"Serve God and your master," said I. "Let his Catholic majesty save me from the hands of the infamous alcalde who has arrested me, an honest and a law-abiding man, who came to Spain trusting in his own innocence and the protection of the laws. The person who writes to you, my lord, has a purse full of doubloons in his pocket; he has already been robbed, and fears assassination in the filthy den in which he has been imprisoned."

I wrote to the Duke of Lossada, requesting him to inform the king that his servants had subjected to vile treatment a man whose only fault was that he had a little money. I begged him to use his influence with his Catholic majesty to put a stop to these infamous proceedings.

But the most vigorous letter of all was the one I addressed to the Count of Aranda. I told him plainly that if this infamous action went on I should be forced to believe that it was by his orders, since I had stated in vain that I came to Madrid with an introduction to him from a princess.

"I have committed no crime," I said; "what compensation am I to have when I am released from this filthy and abominable place?

Set me at liberty at once, or tell your hangmen to finish their work, for I warn you that no one shall take me to the galleys alive."

According to my custom I took copies of all the letters, and I sent them off by the servant whom the all-powerful Manucci despatched to the prison. I passed such a night as Dante might have imagined in his Vision of Hell. All the beds were full, and even if there had been a spare place I would not have occupied it. I asked in vain for a mattress, but even if they had brought me one, it would have been of no use, for the whole floor was inundated. There were only two or three chamber utensils for all the prisoners, and everyone discharged his occasions on the floor.

I spent the night on a narrow bench without a back, resting my head on my hands.

At seven o'clock the next morning Manucci came to see me; I looked upon him as my Providence. I begged him to take me down to the guard-room, and give me some refreshment, for I felt quite exhausted. My request was granted, and as I told my sufferings I had my hair done by a barber.

Manucci told me that my letters would be delivered in the course of the day, and observed, smilingly, that my epistle to the ambassador was rather severe. I shewed him copies of the three others I had written, and the inexperienced young man told me that gentleness was the best way to obtain favours. He did not know that there are circumstances in which a man's pen must be dipped in gall. He told me confidentially that the ambassador dined with Aranda that day, and would speak in my favour as a private individual, adding that he was afraid my letter would prejudice the proud Spaniard against me.

"All I ask of you," said I, "is not to tell the ambassador that you have seen the letter I wrote to the Count of Aranda."

He promised he would keep the secret.

An hour after his departure I saw Donna Ignazia and her father coming in, accompanied by the officer who had treated me with such consideration. Their visit cut me to the quick; nevertheless, I felt grateful, for it shewed me the 'goodness of Don Diego's heart and the love of the fair devotee.

I gave them to understand, in my bad Spanish, that I was grateful for the honour they had done me in visiting me in this dreadful situation. Donna Ignazia did not speak, she only wept in silence; but Don Diego gave me clearly to understand that he would never have come to see me unless he had felt certain that my accusation was a mistake or an infamous calumny. He told me he was sure I should be set free, and that proper satisfaction would be given me.

"I hope so," I replied, "for I am perfectly innocent of any offence." I was greatly touched when the worthy man slipped into my hands a rouleau, telling me it contained twelve quadruples, which I could repay at my convenience.

It was more than a thousand francs, and my hair stood on end. I pressed his hand warmly, and whispered to him that I had fifty in my pocket, which I was afraid to shew him, for fear the rascals around might rob me. He put back his rouleau, and bade me farewell in tears, and I promised to come and see him as soon as I should be set at liberty.

He had not sent in his name, and as he was very well dressed he was taken for a man of importance. Such characters are not altogether exceptional in heroic Spain; it is a land of extremes.

At noon Mengs's servant came with a dinner that was choicer than before, but not so plentiful. This was just what I liked. He waited for me to finish, and went away with the plates, carrying my heartiest thanks to his master.

At one o'clock an individual came up to me and bade me follow him. He took me to a small room, where I saw my carbine and pistols. In front of me was the Alcalde Messa, seated at a table covered with documents, and a policeman stood on each side of him. The alcalde told me to sit down, and to answer truly such questions as might be put to me, warning me that my replies would be taken down.

"I do not understand Spanish well, and I shall only give written answers to any questions that may be asked of me, in Italian, French, or Latin."

This reply, which I uttered in a firm and determined voice, seemed to astonish him. He spoke to me for an hour, and I understood him very well, but he only got one reply:

"I don't understand what you say. Get a judge who understands one of the languages I have named, and I will write down my answers."

The alcalde was enraged, but I did not let his ill-humour or his threats disturb me.

Finally he gave me a pen, and told me to write my name, profession, and business in Spain in Italian. I could not refuse him this pleasure, so I wrote as follows:

"My name is Jacques Casanova; I am a subject of the Republic of Venice, by profession a man of letters, and in rank a Knight of the Golden Spur. I have sufficient means, and I travel for my pleasure. I am known to the Venetian ambassador, the Count of Aranda, the Prince de la Catolica, the Marquis of Moras, and the Duke of Lossada. I have offended in no manner against the laws of his Catholic majesty, but in spite of my innocence I have been cast into a den of thieves and assassins by magistrates who deserve a ten times greater punishment. Since I have not infringed the laws, his Catholic majesty must know that he has only one right over me, and that is to order me to leave his realms, which order I am ready to obey. My arms, which I see before me, have travelled with me for the last eleven years; I carry them to defend myself against highwaymen. They were seen when my effects were examined at the Gate of Alcala, and were not confiscated; which makes it plain that they have served merely as a pretext for the infamous treatment to which I have been subjected."

After I had written out this document I gave it to the alcalde, who called for an interpreter. When he had had it read to him he rose angrily and said to me,—

"Valga me Dios! You shall suffer for your insolence."

With this threat he went away, ordering that I should be taken back to prison.

At eight o'clock Manucci called and told me that the Count of Aranda had been making enquiries about me of the Venetian ambassador, who had spoken very highly in my favour, and expressed his regret that he could not take my part officially on account of my being in disgrace with the State Inquisitors.

"He has certainly been shamefully used," said the count, "but an intelligent man should not lose his head. I should have known nothing about it, but for a furious letter he has written me; and Don Emmanuel de Roda and the Duke of Lossada have received epistles in the same style. Casanova is in the right, but that is not the way to address people."

"If he really said I was in the right, that is sufficient."

"He said it, sure enough."

"Then he must do me justice, and as to my style everyone has a style of their own. I am furious, and I wrote furiously. Look at this place; I have no bed, the floor is covered with filth, and I am obliged to sleep on a narrow bench. Don't you think it is natural that I should desire to eat the hearts of the scoundrels who have placed me here? If I do not leave this hell by tomorrow, I shall kill myself, or go mad."

Manucci understood the horrors of my situation. He promised to come again early the next day, and advised me to see what money would do towards procuring a bed, but I would not listen to him, for I was suffering from injustice, and was therefore obstinate. Besides, the thought of the vermin frightened me, and I was afraid for my purse and the jewels I had about me.

I spent a second night worse than the first, going to sleep from sheer exhaustion, only to awake and find myself slipping off the bench.

Manucci came before eight o'clock, and my aspect shocked him. He had come in his carriage, bringing with him some excellent chocolate, which in some way restored my spirits. As I was finishing it, an officer of high rank, accompanied by two other officers, came in and called out,—

"M. de Casanova!"

I stepped forward and presented myself.

"Chevalier," he began, "the Count of Aranda is at the gate of the prison; he is much grieved at the treatment you have received. He only heard about it through the letter you wrote him yesterday, and if you had written sooner your pains would have been shorter."

"Such was my intention, colonel, but a soldier . . . ."

I proceeded to tell him the story of the swindling soldier, and on hearing his name the colonel called the captain of the guard, reprimanded him severely, and ordered him to give me back the crown himself. I took the money laughingly, and the colonel then ordered the captain to fetch the offending soldier, and to give him a flogging before me.

This officer, the emissary of the all-powerful Aranda, was Count Royas, commanding the garrison of Buen Retiro. I told him all the circumstances of my arrest, and of my imprisonment in that filthy place. I told him that if I did not get back that day my arms, my liberty, and my honour, I should either go mad or kill myself.

"Here," I said, "I can neither rest nor sleep, and a man needs sleep every night. If you had come a little earlier you would have seen the disgusting filth with which the floor was covered."

The worthy man was taken aback with the energy with which I spoke. I saw his feelings, and hastened to say,—

"You must remember, colonel, that I am suffering from injustice, and am in a furious rage. I am a man of honour, like yourself, and you can imagine the effect of such treatment on me."

Manucci told him, in Spanish, that in my normal state I was a good fellow enough. The colonel expressed his pity for me, and assured me that my arms should be restored to me, and my liberty too, in the course of the day.

"Afterwards," said he, "you must go and thank his excellency the Count of Aranda, who came here expressly for your sake. He bade me tell you that your release would be delayed till the afternoon, that you may have full satisfaction for the affront you have received, if it is an affront, for the penalties of the law only dishonour the guilty. In this instance the Alcalde Messa has been deceived by the rascal who was in your service."

"There he is," said I. "Be good enough to have him removed, or else, in my indignation, I might kill him."

"He shall be taken away this moment," he replied.

The colonel went out, and two minutes later two soldiers came in and took the rogue away between them. I never saw him again, and never troubled myself to enquire what had become of him.

The colonel begged me to accompany him to the guard-room, to see the thieving soldier flogged. Manucci was at my side, and at some little distance stood the Count of Aranda, surrounded by officers, and accompanied by a royal guard.

The business kept us there for a couple of hours. Before leaving me the colonel begged me to meet Mengs at dinner at his house.

When I returned to my filthy prison I found a clean arm-chair, which I was informed had been brought in for me. I sat down in it immediately, and Manucci left me, after embracing me again and again. He was my sincere friend, and I can never forgive myself the stupidity which made me offend him grievously. He never forgave me, at which I am not surprised, but I believe my readers will agree with me in thinking that he carried his vengeance too far.

After the scene which had taken place, the vile crowd of prisoners stood gazing at me in stupid silence, and Marazzini came up to me and begged me to use my offices for him.

Dinner was brought me as usual, and at three o'clock the Alcalde Messa appeared and begged me to follow him, as he had received orders to take me back to my lodging, where he hoped I should find everything in perfect order. At the same time he shewed me my arms, which one of his men was going to bring to my house. The officer of the guard returned me my sword, the alcalde, who was in his black cloak, put himself on my left hand, and thus I was escorted home with a guard of thirty constables. The seals were removed from my apartment, and after a brief inspection I pronounced that everything was in perfect order.

"If you had not a rascal and a traitor (who shall end his days in the galleys) in your service, Senor Caballero, you would never have written down the servants of his Catholic majesty as scoundrels."

"Senor Alcalde, my indignation made me write the same sentence to four of his majesty's ministers. Then I believed what I wrote, but I do so no longer. Let us forget and forgive; but you must confess that if I had not known how to write a letter you would have sent me to the galleys."

"Alas! it is very likely."

I need not say that I hastened to remove all traces of the vile prison where I had suffered so much. When I was ready to go out my first grateful visit was paid to the noble cobbler. The worthy man was proud of the fulfilment of his prophecy, and glad to see me again. Donna Ignazia was wild with delight—perhaps she had not been so sure of my release—and when Don Diego heard of the satisfaction that had been given me he said that a grandee of Spain could not have asked for more. I begged the worthy people to come and dine with me, telling them that I would name the day another time, and they accepted gladly.

I felt that my love for Donna Ignazia had increased immensely since our last meeting.

Afterwards I called on Mengs, who with his knowledge of Spanish law expected nothing less than to see me. When he heard of my triumphant release he overwhelmed me with congratulations. He was in his Court dress—an unusual thing with him, and on my asking him the reason he told me that he had been to Don Emmanuel de Roda's to speak on my behalf, but had not succeeded in obtaining an audience. He gave me a Venetian letter which had just arrived for me. I opened it, and found it was from M. Dandolo, and contained an enclosure for M. de Mocenigo. M. Dandolo said that on reading the enclosed letter the ambassador would have no more scruples about introducing me, as it contained a recommendation from one of the Inquisitors on behalf of the three.

When I told Mengs of this he said it was now in my power to make my fortune in Spain, and that now was the time when all the ministers would be only too anxious to do something for me to make me forget the wrongs I had received.

"I advise you," he said, "to take the letter to the ambassador immediately. Take my carriage; after what you have undergone for the last few days you cannot be in a walking humour."

I had need of rest, and told Mengs that I would not sup with him that night, but would dine with him the next day. The ambassador was out, so I left the letter with Manucci, and then drove home and slept profoundly for twelve hours.

Manucci came to see me the next day in high spirits, and told me that M. Girolamo Zulian had written to the ambassador on behalf of M. du Mula, informing him that he need not hesitate to countenance me, as any articles the Tribunal might have against me were in no degree prejudicial to my honour.

"The ambassador," he continued, "proposes to introduce you at Court next week, and he wants you to dine with him to-day; there will be a numerous company at dinner."

"I am engaged to Mengs."

"No matter, he shall be asked as well; you must come. Consider the effect of your presence at the ambassador's the day after your triumph."

"You are right. Go and ask Mengs, and tell the ambassador that I have much pleasure in accepting his invitation."

CHAPTER V

Campomanes—Olavides—Sierra Morena—Aranjuez—Mengs—
The Marquis Grimaldi—Toledo—Madame Pelliccia—My Return
to Madrid

Different circumstances in my life seem to have combined to
render me somewhat superstitious; it is a humiliating confession,
and yet I make it. But who could help it? A man who abandons
himself to his whims and fancies is like a child playing with a
billiard cue. It may make a stroke that would be an honour to the
most practised and scientific player; and such are the strange
coincidences of life which, as I have said, have caused me to become
superstitious.

Fortune, which under the humbler name of luck seems but a word,
is a very divinity when it guides the most important actions of a
man's life. Always it has seemed to me that this divinity is not
blind, as the mythologists affirm; she had brought me low only to
exalt me, and I found myself in high places, only, as it seems, to
be cast into the depths. Fortune has done her best to make me
regard her as a reasoning, almighty power; she has made me feel
that the strength of my will is as nothing before this mysterious
power, which takes my will and moulds it, and makes it a mere
instrument for the accomplishment of its decrees.

I could not possibly have done anything in Spain without the help
of the representative of my country, and he would not have dared
to do anything for me without the letter I had just given him. This
letter, in its turn, would probably have had but slight effect if it

had not come to hand so soon after my imprisonment, which had become the talk of the town, through the handsome satisfaction the Count of Aranda had given me.

The letter made the ambassador sorry that he had not interposed on my behalf, but he hoped people would believe that the count would not have acted as he did if it had not been for his interposition. His favourite, Count Manucci, had come to ask me to dinner; as it happened I was engaged to Mengs, which obtained an invitation for the painter, and flattered his vanity excessively. He fancied that the invitation proceeded from gratitude, and it certainly smoothed away the mortification he had felt at seeing me arrested in his house. He immediately wrote to the effect that he would call upon me with his carriage.

I called on the Count of Aranda, who kept me waiting for a quarter of an hour, and then came in with some papers in his hand. He smiled when he saw me, and said,—

"Your business is done. Stay, here are four letters; take them and read them over again."

"Why should I read them again? This is the document I gave the alcalde."

"I know that. Read, and confess that you should not have written so violently, in spite of the wrongs that vexed you."

"I crave your pardon, my lord, but a man who meditates suicide does not pick terms. I believed that your excellency was at the bottom of it all."

"Then you don't know me. Go and thank Don Emmanuel de Roda, who wants to know you, and I shall be glad if you will call once on the alcalde, not to make him an apology, for you owe him none, but as an act of politeness to salve over the hard things you said of him. If you write the history of Princess Lubomirska, I hope you will tell her that I did my best for you."

I then called on Colonel Royas, who told me that I had made a great mistake in saying that I was satisfied.

"What could I claim?"

"Everything. Dismissal of the alcalde and compensation to the tune of fifty thousand duros. Spain is a country where a man may speak out save in the matters which the Holy Inquisition looks after."

This colonel, now a general, is one of the pleasantest Spaniards I have ever met.

I had not long returned to my lodging when Mengs called for me in his carriage. The ambassador gave me a most gracious reception, and overwhelmed Mengs with compliments for having endeavoured to shelter me. At dinner I told the story of my sufferings at Buen Retiro, and the conversation I had just had with the Count of Aranda, who had returned me my letters. The company expressed a desire to see them, and everyone gave an opinion on the matter.

The guests were Abbe Bigliardi, the French consul, Don Rodrigues de Campomanes, and the famous Don Pablo d'Olavides. Everyone spoke his mind, and the ambassador condemned the letters as too ferocious. On the other hand, Campomanes approved them, saying that they were not abusive, and were wonderfully adapted to my purpose, namely, to force the reader to do me prompt justice, were the reader to be the king himself. Olavides and Bigliardi echoed this sentiment. Mengs sided with the ambassador, and begged me to come and live with him, so as not to be liable to any more inconveniences from spying servants. I did not accept this invitation till I had been pressed for some time, and I noted the remark of the ambassador, who said I owed Mengs this reparation for the indirect affront he had received.

I was delighted to make the acquaintance of Campomanes and Olavides, men of intellect and of a stamp very rare in Spain. They were not exactly men of learning, but they were above religious prejudices, and were not only fearless in throwing public scorn upon them but even laboured openly for their destruction. It was Campomanes who had furnished Aranda with all the damaging matter against the Jesuits. By a curious coincidence, Campomanes, the Count of Aranda, and the General of the Jesuits, were all squint-eyed. I asked Campomanes why he hated the Jesuits so bitterly, and he replied that he looked upon them in the same light as the other religious orders, whom he considered a parasitical and noxious race, and would gladly banish them all, not only from the peninsula but from the face of the earth.

He was the author of all the pamphlets that had been written on the subject of mortmain; and as he was an intimate friend of the ambassador's, M. Mocenigo had furnished him with an account of the proceedings of the Venetian Republic against the monks. He might have dispensed with this source of information if he had read the writings of Father Paul Sarpi on the same subject. Quick-sighted, firm, with the courage of his opinions, Campomanes was the fiscal of the Supreme Council of Castille, of which Aranda was president. Everyone knew him to be a thoroughly honest man, who acted solely for the good of the State. Thus statesmen and officials had warm feelings of respect for him, while the monks and bigots hated the sound of his name, and the Inquisition had sworn to be his ruin. It was said openly that he would either become a bishop or perish in the cells of the holy brotherhood. The prophecy was only partly fulfilled. Four years after my visit to Spain he was incarcerated in the dungeons of the Inquisition, but he obtained his release after three years' confinement by doing public penance. The leprosy which eats out the heart of Spain is not yet cured. Olavides was still more harshly treated, and even Aranda would have fallen a victim if he had not had the good sense to ask the king to send him to France as his ambassador. The king was very glad to do so, as otherwise he would have been forced to deliver him up to the infuriated monks. Charles III. (who died a madman) was a remarkable character. He was as obstinate as a mule, as weak as a woman, as gross as a Dutchman, and a thorough-paced bigot. It was no wonder that he became the tool of his confessor.

At the time of which I am speaking the cabinet of Madrid was occupied in a curious scheme. A thousand Catholic families had been enticed from Switzerland to form a colony in the beautiful but deserted region called the Sierra Morena, well known all over Europe by its mention in Don Quixote. Nature seemed there to have lavished all her gifts; the climate was perfect, the soil fertile, and streams of all kinds watered the land, but in spite of all it was almost depopulated.

Desiring to change this state of things, his Catholic majesty had decided to make a present of all the agricultural products for a certain number of years to industrious colonists. He had consequently invited the Swiss Catholics, and had paid their expenses for the journey. The Swiss arrived, and the Spanish government did its best to provide them with lodging and spiritual and temporal superintendence. Olavides was the soul of this scheme. He conferred with the ministers to provide the new population with magistrates, priests, a governor, craftsmen of all kinds to build churches and houses, and especially a bull-ring, a necessity for the Spaniards, but a perfectly useless provision as far as the simple Swiss were concerned.

In the documents which Don Pablo Olavides had composed on the subject he demonstrated the inexpediency of establishing any religious orders in the new colony, but if he could have proved his opinion to be correct with foot and rule he would none the less have drawn on his head the implacable hatred of the monks, and of the bishop in whose diocese the new colony was situated. The secular clergy supported Olavides, but the monks cried out against his impiety, and as the Inquisition was eminently monkish in its sympathies persecution had already begun, and this was one of the subjects of conversation at the dinner at which I was present.

I listened to the arguments, sensible and otherwise, which were advanced, and I finally gave my opinion, as modestly as I could, that in a few years the colony would banish like smoke; and this for several reasons.

"The Swiss," I said, "are a very peculiar people; if you transplant them to a foreign shore, they languish and die; they become a prey to home-sickness. When this once begins in a Switzer, the only thing is to take him home to the mountain, the lake, or the valley, where he was born, or else he will infallibly die."

"It would be wise, I think," I continued, "to endeavour to combine a Spanish colony with the Swiss colony, so as to effect a mingling of races. At first, at all events, their rules, both spiritual and temporal, should be Swiss, and, above all, you would have to insure them complete immunity from the Inquisition. The Swiss who has been bred in the country has peculiar customs and manners of love-making, of which the Spanish Church might not exactly approve; but the least attempt to restrain their liberty in this respect would immediately bring about a general home-sickness."

At first Olavides thought I was joking, but he soon found out that my remarks had some sense in them. He begged me to write out my opinions on the subject, and to give him the benefit of my knowledge. I promised to do so, and Mengs fixed a day for him to come and dine with me at his house.

The next day I moved my household goods to Mengs's house, and began my philosophical and physiological treatise on the colony.

I called on Don Emmanuel de Roda, who was a man of letters, a 'rara aves' in Spain. He liked Latin poetry, had read some Italian, but very naturally gave the palm to the Spanish poets. He welcomed me warmly, begged me to come and see him again, and told me how sorry he had been at my unjust imprisonment.

The Duke of Lossada congratulated me on the way in which the Venetian ambassador spoke of me everywhere, and encouraged me in my idea of getting some place under Government, promising to give me his support in the matter.

The Prince della Catolica, invited me to dinner with the Venetian ambassador; and in the course of three weeks I had made a great number of valuable acquaintances. I thought seriously of seeking employment in Spain, as not having heard from Lisbon I dared not go there on the chance of finding something to do. I had not received any letters from Pauline of late, and had no idea as to what had become of her.

I passed a good many of my evenings with a Spanish lady, named Sabatini, who gave 'tertullas' or assemblies, frequented chiefly by fifth-rate literary men. I also visited the Duke of Medina-Sidonia, a well-read and intelligent man, to whom I had been presented by Don Domingo Varnier, one of the gentlemen of the king's chamber, whom I had met at Mengs's house. I paid a good many visits to Donna Ignazia, but as I was never left alone with her these visits became tiresome. When I suggested a party of pleasure with her and her cousins, she replied that she would like it as much as I, but as it was Lent and near Holy Week, in which God died for our salvation, it was more fit to think of penance than pleasure. After Easter, she said, we might consider the matter. Ignazia was a perfect example of the young Spanish devotee.

A fortnight after, the King and Court left Madrid for Aranjuez. M. de Mocenigo asked me to come and stay with him, as he would be able to present me at Court. As may be imagined, I should have been only too glad to accept, but on the eve of my departure, as I was driving with Mengs, I was suddenly seized with a fever, and was convulsed so violently that my head was dashed against the carriage window, which it shivered to fragments. Mengs ordered the coachman to drive home, and I was put to bed. In four hours I was seized with a sweating fit, which lasted for ten or twelve hours. The bed and two mattresses were soaked through with my perspiration, which dripped on to the floor beneath. The fever abated in forty-eight hours, but left me in such a state of weakness that I was kept to my bed for a whole week, and could not go to Aranjuez till Holy Saturday. The ambassador welcomed me warmly, but on the night I arrived a small lump which I had felt in the course of the day grew as large as an egg, and I was unable to go to mass on Easter Day.

In five days the excrescence became as large as an average melon, much to the amazement of Manucci and the ambassador, and even of the king's surgeon, a Frenchman who declared he had never seen the like before. I was not alarmed personally, for, as I suffered no pain and the lump was quite soft, I guessed it was only a collection of lymph, the remainder of the evil humours which I had sweated away in the fever. I told the surgeon the history of the fever and begged him to lance the abscess, which he did, and for four days the opening discharged an almost incredible amount of matter. On the fifth day the wound was almost healed, but the exhaustion had left me so weak that I could not leave my bed.

Such was my situation when I received a letter from Mengs. It is before me at the present moment, and I give below a true copy:

"Yesterday the rector of the parish in which I reside affixed to the church-door a list of those of his parishioners who are Atheists and have neglected their Easter duties. Amongst them your name figures in full, and the aforesaid rector has reproached me bitterly for harbouring a heretic. I did not know what answer to make, for I feel sure that you could have stopped in Madrid a day longer to discharge the duties of a Christian, even if it were only out of regard for me. The duty I owe to the king, my master, the care I am bound to take of my reputation, and my fears of being molested, all make me request you to look upon my house as yours no longer. When you return to Madrid you may go where you will, and my servants shall transport your effects to your new abode.

"I am, etc.,
"ANTONIO RAPHAEL MENGS."

I was so annoyed by this rude, brutal, and ungrateful letter, that if I had not been seven leagues from Madrid, and in a state of the utmost weakness, Mengs should have suffered for his insolence. I told the messenger who had brought it to begone, but he replied that he had orders to await my reply. I crushed the letter in my hand and flung it at his face, saying,—

"Go and tell your unworthy master what I did with his letter, and tell him that is the only answer that such a letter deserves."

The innocent messenger went his way in great amazement.

My anger gave me strength, and having dressed myself and summoned a sedan-chair I went to church, and was confessed by a Grey Friar, and at six o'clock the next morning I received the Sacrament.

My confessor was kind enough to give me a certificate to the effect that I had been obliged to keep my bed since my arrival 'al sitio', and that in spite of my extreme weakness I had gone to church, and had confessed and communicated like a good Christian. He also told me the name of the priest who had affixed the paper containing my name to the door of the church.

When I returned to the ambassador's house I wrote to this priest, telling him that the certificate enclosed would inform him as to my reasons for not communicating. I expressed a hope that, being satisfied of my orthodoxy, he would not delay in removing my name from his church-doors, and I concluded by begging him to hand the enclosed letter to the Chevalier Mengs.

To the painter I wrote that I felt that I had deserved the shameful insult he had given me by my great mistake in acceding to his request to honour him by staying in his house. However, as a good Christian who had just received the Holy Communion, I told him that his brutal behaviour was forgiven; but I bade him to take to heart the line, well known to all honest people, and doubtless unknown to him:

'Turpius ejicitur quam non admittitur hospes.'

After sending the letter I told the ambassador what had happened, to which he replied,—

"I am not at all surprised at what you tell me. Mengs is only liked for his talents in painting; in everything else he is well known to be little better than a fool."

As a matter of fact he had only asked me to stay with him to gratify his own vanity. He knew that all the town was talking of my imprisonment and of the satisfaction the Count of Aranda had accorded me, and he wanted people to think that his influence had obtained the favour that had been shewn me. Indeed, he had said in a moment of exaltation that I should have compelled the Alcade Messa to escort me not to my own house but to his, as it was in his house that I had been arrested.

Mengs was an exceedingly ambitious and a very jealous man; he hated all his brother painters. His colour and design were excellent, but his invention was very weak, and invention is as necessary to a great painter as a great poet.

I happened to say to him one day, "Just as every poet should be a painter, so every painter should be a poet;" and he got quite angry, thinking that I was alluding to his weakness of imagination, which he felt but would not acknowledge.

He was an ignorant man, and liked to pass for a scholar; he sacrificed to Bacchus and Comus, and would fain be thought sober; he was lustful, bad-tempered, envious, and miserly, but yet would be considered a virtuous man. He loved hard work, and this forced him to abstain, as a rule, from dinner, as he drank so inordinately at that meal that he could do nothing after it. When he dined out he had to drink nothing but water, so as not to compromise his reputation for temperance. He spoke four languages, and all badly, and could not even write his native tongue with correctness; and yet he claimed perfection for his grammar and orthography, as for all his other qualities. While I was staying with him I became acquainted with some of his weak points, and endeavoured to correct them, at which he took great offence. The fellow writhed under a sense of obligation to me. Once I prevented his sending a petition to the Court, which the king would have seen, and which would have made Mengs ridiculous. In signing his name he had written 'el mas inclito', wishing to say your most humble. I pointed out to him that 'el mas inclito' meant the most illustrious, and that the Spanish for the expression he wanted was 'el mas humilde'. The proud fool was quite enraged, telling me that he knew Spanish better than I, but when the dictionary was searched he had to swallow the bitter pill of confessing himself in the wrong.

Another time I suppressed a heavy and stupid criticism of his on someone who had maintained that there were no monuments still existing of the antediluvian period. Mengs thought he would confound the author by citing the remains of the Tower of Babel— a double piece of folly, for in the first place there are no such remains, and in the second, the Tower of Babel was a post-diluvian building.

He was also largely given to the discussion of metaphysical questions, on which his knowledge was simply nil, and a favourite pursuit of his was defining beauty in the abstract, and when he was on this topic the nonsense he talked was something dreadful.

Mengs was a very passionate man, and would sometimes beat his children most cruelly. More than once I have rescued his poor sons from his furious hands. He boasted that his father, a bad Bohemian artist, had brought him up with the stick. Thus, he said, he had become a great painter, and he wished his own children to enjoy the same advantages.

He was deeply offended when he received a letter, of which the address omitted his title of chevalier, and his name, Rafael. One day I ventured to say that these things were but trifles after all, and that I had taken no offence at his omitting the chevalier on the letters he had written to me, though I was a knight of the same order as himself. He very wisely made no answer; but his objection to the omission of his baptismal name was a very ridiculous one. He said he was called Antonio after Antonio Correggio, and Rafael after Rafael da Urbino, and that those who omitted these names, or either of them, implicitly denied his possession of the qualities of both these great painters.

Once I dared to tell him that he had made a mistake in the hand of one of his figures, as the ring finger was shorter than the index. He replied sharply that it was quite right, and shewed me his hand by way of proof. I laughed, and shewed him my hand in return, saying that I was certain that my hand was made like that of all the descendants of Adam.

"Then whom do you think that I am descended from?"

"I don't know, but you are certainly not of the same species as myself."

"You mean you are not of my species; all well-made hands of men, and women too, are like mine and not like yours."

"I'll wager a hundred doubloons that you are in the wrong."

He got up, threw down brushes and palette, and rang up his servants, saying,—

"We shall see which is right."

The servants came, and on examination he found that I was right. For once in his life, he laughed and passed it off as a joke, saying,—

"I am delighted that I can boast of being unique in one particular, at all events."

Here I must note another very sensible remark of his.

He had painted a Magdalen, which was really wonderfully beautiful. For ten days he had said every morning, "The picture will be finished to-night." At last I told him that he had made a mistake in saying it would be finished, as he was still working on it.

"No, I have not," he replied, "ninety-nine connoisseurs out of a hundred would have pronounced it finished long ago, but I want the praise of the hundredth man. There's not a picture in the world that can be called finished save in a relative sense; this Magdalen will not be finished till I stop working at it, and then it will be only finished relatively, for if I were to give another day's work to it it would be more finished still. Not one of Petrarch's sonnets is a really finished production; no, nor any other man's sonnets. Nothing that the mind of man can conceive is perfect, save it be a mathematical theorem."

I expressed my warm approval of the excellent way in which he had spoken.
He was not so sensible another time when he expressed a wish to have been
Raphael.

"He was such a great painter."

"Certainly," said I, "but what can you mean by wishing you had been Raphael? This is not sense; if you had been Raphael, you would no longer be existing. But perhaps you only meant to express a wish that you were tasting the joys of Paradise; in that case I will say no more."

"No, no; I mean I would have liked to have been Raphael without troubling myself about existing now, either in soul or body."

"Really such a desire is an absurdity; think it over, and you will see it for yourself."

He flew into a rage, and abused me so heartily that I could not help laughing.

Another time he made a comparison between a tragic author and a painter, of course to the advantage of the latter.

I analysed the matter calmly, shewing him that the painter's labour is to a great extent purely mechanical, and can be done whilst engaged in casual talk; whilst a well-written tragedy is the work of genius pure and simple. Therefore, the poet must be immeasurably superior to the painter.

"Find me if you can," said I, "a poet who can order his supper between the lines of his tragedy, or discuss the weather whilst he is composing epic verses."

When Mengs was beaten in an argument, instead of acknowledging his defeat, he invariably became brutal and insulting. He died at the age of fifty, and is regarded by posterity as a Stoic philosopher, a scholar, and a compendium of all the virtues; and this opinion must be ascribed to a fine biography of him in royal quarto, choicely printed, and dedicated to the King of Spain. This panegyric is a mere tissue of lies. Mengs was a great painter, and nothing else; and if he had only produced the splendid picture which hangs over the high altar of the chapel royal at Dresden, he would deserve eternal fame, though indeed he is indebted to the great Raphael for the idea of the painting.

We shall hear more of Mengs when I describe my meeting with him at Rome, two or three years later.

I was still weak and confined to my room when Manucci came to me, and proposed that I should go with him to Toledo.

"The ambassador," he said, "is going to give a grand official dinner to the ambassadors of the other powers, and as I have not been presented at Court I am excluded from being present. However, if I travel, my absence will not give rise to any remarks. We shall be back in five or six days."

I was delighted to have the chance of seeing Toledo, and of making the journey in a comfortable carriage, so I accepted. We started the next morning, and reached Toledo in the evening of the same day. For Spain we were lodged comfortably enough, and the next day we went out under the charge of a cicerone, who took us to the Alcazar, the Louvre of Toledo, formerly the palace of the Moorish kings. Afterwards we inspected the cathedral, which is well worthy of a visit, on account of the riches it contains. I saw the great tabernacle used on Corpus Christi. It is made of silver, and is so heavy that it requires thirty strong men to lift it. The Archbishop of Toledo has three hundred thousand duros a year, and his clergy have four hundred thousand, amounting to two million francs in French money. One of the canons, as he was shewing me the urns containing the relics, told me that one of them contained the thirty pieces of silver for which Judas betrayed our Lord. I begged him to let me see them, to which he replied severely that the king himself would not have dared to express such indecent curiosity.

I hastened to apologise, begging him not to take offence at a stranger's heedless questions; and this seemed to calm his anger.

The Spanish priests are a band of knaves, but one has to treat them with more respect than one would pay to honest men elsewhere. The following day we were shewn the museum of natural history. It was rather a dull exhibition; but, at all events, one could laugh at it without exciting the wrath of the monks and the terrors of the Inquisition. We were shewn, amongst other wonders, a stuffed dragon, and the man who exhibited it said,—

"This proves, gentlemen, that the dragon is not a fabulous animal;" but I thought there was more of art than nature about the beast. He then shewed us a basilisk, but instead of slaying us with a glance it only made us laugh. The greatest wonder of all, however, was nothing else than a Freemason's apron, which, as the curator very sagely declared, proved the existence of such an order, whatever some might say.

The journey restored me to health, and when I returned to Aranjuez, I proceeded to pay my court to all the ministers. The ambassador presented me to Marquis Grimaldi, with whom I had some conversations on the subject of the Swiss colony, which was going on badly. I reiterated my opinion that the colony should be composed of Spaniards.

"Yes," said he, "but Spain is thinly peopled everywhere, and your plan would amount to impoverishing one district to make another rich."

"Not at all, for if you took ten persons who are dying of poverty in the Asturias, and placed them in the Sierra Morena, they would not die till they had begotten fifty children. This fifty would beget two hundred and so on."

My scheme was laid before a commission, and the marquis promised that I should be made governor of the colony if the plan was accepted.

An Italian Opera Comique was then amusing the Court, with the exception of the king, who had no taste for music. His majesty bore a considerable resemblance to a sheep in the face, and it seemed as if the likeness went deeper, for sheep have not the slightest idea of sound. His favourite pursuit was sport, and the reason will be given later on.

An Italian musician at the Court desired to compose some music for a new opera, and as there was no time to send to Italy I offered to compose the libretto. My offer was accepted, and by the next day the first act was ready. The music was composed in four days, and the Venetian ambassador invited all the ministers to the rehearsal in the grand hall of his palace. The music was pronounced exquisite; the two other acts were written, and in a fortnight the opera was put upon the stage. The musician was rewarded handsomely, but I was considered too grand to work for money and my reward was paid me in the Court money of compliments. However, I was glad to see that the ambassador was proud of me and that the minister's esteem for me seemed increased.

In writing the libretto I had become acquainted with the actresses. The chief of them was a Roman named Pelliccia, neither pretty nor ugly, with a slight squint, and but moderate talents. Her younger sister was pretty if not handsome; but no one cared for the younger, while the elder was a universal favourite. Her expression was pleasant, her smile delightful, and her manners most captivating. Her husband was an indifferent painter, plain-looking, and more like her servant than her husband. He was indeed her very humble servant, and she treated him with great kindness. The feelings she inspired me with were not love, but a sincere respect and friendship. I used to visit her every day, and wrote verses for her to sing to the Roman airs she delivered so gracefully.

On one of the days of rehearsals I was pointing out to her the various great personages who were present. The manager of the company, Marescalchi by name, had entered into an arrangement with the Governor of Valentia to bring the company there in September to play comic opera in a small theatre which had been built on purpose. Italian opera had hitherto never been presented at Valentia, and Marecalchi hoped to make a good deal of money there. Madame Pelliccia knew nobody in Valentia, and wanted a letter of introduction to someone there. She asked me if I thought she could venture to ask the Venetian ambassador to do her the favour, but I advised her to try the Duke of Arcos.

"Where is he?"

"That gentleman who is looking in your direction now."

"How can I dare to ask him?"

"He is a true nobleman, and I am sure he will be only too happy to oblige you. Go and ask him now; you will not be denied."

"I haven't the courage to do so. Come with me and introduce me."

"That would spoil everything; he must not even think that I am your adviser in the matter. I am just going to leave you; you must make your request directly afterwards."

I walked towards the orchestra, and looking round I saw that the duke was approaching the actress.

"The thing's as good as done," I said to myself.

After the rehearsal was over Madame Pelliccia came and told me that the Duke would give her the letter on the day on which the opera was produced. He kept his word, and she received a sealed letter for a merchant and banker, Don Diego Valencia.

It was then May, and she was not to go to Valentia till September, so we shall hear what the letter contained later on.

I often saw the king's gentleman of the chamber, Don Domingo Varnier, another 'gentleman in the service of the Princess of the Asturias, and one of the princess's bed-chamber women. This most popular princess succeeded in suppressing a good deal of the old etiquette, and the tone of her Court had lost the air of solemnity common in Spanish society. It was a strange thing to see the King of Spain always dining at eleven o'clock, like the Parisian cordwainers in the seventeenth century. His meal always consisted of the same dishes, he always went out hunting at the same hour, coming back in the evening thoroughly fatigued.

The king was ugly, but everything is relative, he was handsome compared with his brother, who was terrifically ugly.

This brother never went anywhere without a picture of the Virgin, which Mengs had painted for him. It was two feet high by three and a half broad. The figure was depicted as seated on the grass with legs crossed after the Eastern fashion, and uncovered up to the knees. It was, in reality, a voluptuous painting; and the prince mistook for devotion that which was really a sinful passion, for it was impossible to look upon the figure without desiring to have the original within one's arms. However, the prince did not see this, and was delighted to find himself in love with the mother of the Saviour. In this he was a true Spaniard; they only love pictures of this kind, and interpret the passions they excite in the most favourable sense.

At Madrid I had, seen a picture of the Madonna with the child at her breast. It was the altarpiece of a chapel in the Calle St. Jeronimo. The place was filled all day by the devout, who came to adore the Mother of God, whose figure was only interesting by reason of her magnificent breast. The alms given at this chapel were so numerous, that in the hundred and fifty years, since the picture had been placed there, the clergy had been able to purchase numerous lamps and candlesticks of silver, and vessels of silver gilt, and even of gold. The doorway was always blocked by carriages, and a sentinel was placed there to keep order amongst the coachmen; no nobleman would pass by without going in to pray to the Virgin, and to contemplate those 'beata ubera, quae lactaverunt aeterni patris filium'. But there came a change.

When I returned to Madrid I wanted to pay a visit to the Abbe Pico, and told my coachman to take another way so as to avoid the crush in front of the chapel.

"It is not so frequented now, senor," said he, "I can easily get by it."

He went on his way, and I found the entrance to the chapel deserted. As I was getting out of the carriage I asked my coachman what was the reason of the change, and he replied,—

"Oh, senor! men are getting more wicked every day."

This reason did not satisfy me, and when I had taken my chocolate with the abbe, an intelligent and venerable old man, I asked him why the chapel in question had lost its reputation.

He burst out laughing, and replied,—

"Excuse me, I really cannot tell you. Go and see for yourself; your curiosity will soon be satisfied."

As soon as I left him I went to the chapel, and the state of the picture told me all. The breast of the Virgin had disappeared under a kerchief which some profane brush had dared to paint over it. The beautiful picture was spoilt; the magic and fascination had disappeared. Even the teat had been painted out; the Child held on to nothing, and the head of the Virgin no longer appeared natural.

This disaster had taken place at the end of the Carnival of 1768. The old chaplain died, and the Vandal who succeeded him pronounced the painting to be a scandalous one, and robbed it of all its charm.

He may have been in the right as a fool, but as a Christian and a Spaniard he was certainly in the wrong, and he was probably soon convinced of the mistake he had made by the diminution in the offerings of the faithful.

My interest in the study of human nature made me call on this priest, whom I expected to find a stupid old man.

I went one morning, but instead of being old, the priest was an active, clever-looking man of thirty, who immediately offered me chocolate with the best grace imaginable. I refused, as was my duty as a stranger, and indeed the Spaniards offer visitors chocolate so frequently at all hours, that if one accepted it all one would be choked.

I lost no time in exordiums, but came to the point at once, by saying that as a lover of paintings I had been grieved at finding the magnificent Madonna spoilt.

"Very likely," he replied, "but it was exactly the physical beauty of the picture that rendered it in my eyes unfit to represent one whose aspect should purify and purge the senses, instead of exciting them. Let all the pictures in the world be destroyed, if they be found to have caused the commission of one mortal sin."

"Who allowed you to commit this mutilation? The Venetian State Inquisitors, even M. Barberigo, though he is a devout man, would have put you under the Leads for such a deed. The love of Paradise should not be allowed to interfere with the fine arts, and I am sure that St. Luke himself (who was a painter, as you know) would condemn you if he could come to life again."

"Sir, I needed no one's leave or license. I have to say mass at that altar every day, and I am not ashamed to tell you that I was unable to consecrate. You are a man and a Christian, you can excuse my weakness. That voluptuous picture drew away my thoughts from holy things."

"Who obliged you to look at it?"

"I did not look at it; the devil, the enemy of God, made me see it in spite of myself."

"Then you should have mutilated yourself like Origen. Your generative organs, believe me, are not so valuable as the picture you have ruined."

"Sir, you insult me."

"Not at all, I have no intention of doing so."

That young priest shewed me the door with such brusqueness that I felt sure he would inform against me to the Inquisition. I knew he would have no difficulty in finding out my name, so I resolved to be beforehand with him.

Both my fear and my resolve were inspired by an incident which I shall mention as an episode.

A few days before, I had met a Frenchman named Segur, who had just come out of the prisons of the Inquisition. He had been shut up for three years for committing the following crime:

In the hall of his house there was a fountain, composed of a marble basin and the statue of a naked child, who discharged the water in the same way as the well-known statue of Brussels, that is to say, by his virile member. The child might be a Cupid or an Infant Jesus, as you pleased, but the sculptor had adorned the head with a kind of aureole; and so the fanatics declared that it was a mocking of God.

Poor Segur was accused of impiety, and the Inquisition dealt with him accordingly.

I felt that my fault might be adjudged as great as Segur's, and not caring to run the risk of a like punishment I called on the bishop, who held the office of Grand Inquisitor, and told him word for word the conversation I had had with the iconoclast chaplain. I ended by craving pardon, if I had offended the chaplain, as I was a good Christian, and orthodox on all points.

I had never expected to find the Grand Inquisitor of Madrid a kindly and intelligent, though ill-favoured, prelate; but so it was, and he did nothing but laugh from the beginning to the end of my story, for he would not let me call it a confession.

"The chaplain," he said, "is himself blameworthy and unfit for his position, in that he has adjudged others to be as weak as himself; in fact, he has committed a wrong against religion. Nevertheless, my dear son, it was not wise of you to go and irritate him." As I had told him my name he shewed me, smilingly, an accusation against me, drawn up by someone who had witnessed the fact. The good bishop gently chid me for having called the friar-confessor of the Duke of Medina an ignoramus. He had refused to admit that a priest might say mass a second time on a high festival, after breaking his fast, on the command of his sovereign prince, who, by the hypothesis, had not heard mass before.

"You were quite right in your contention," said the Inquisitor, "but yet every truth is not good to utter, and it was wrong to call the man an ignoramus in his presence. For the future you would do well to avoid all idle discussion on religious matters, both on dogma and discipline. And I must also tell you, in order that you may not leave Spain with any harsh ideas on the Inquisition, that the priest who affixed your name to the church-door amongst the excommunicated has been severely reprimanded. He ought to have given you a fatherly admonition, and, above all, enquired as to your health, as we know that you were seriously ill at the time."

Thereupon I knelt down and kissed his hand, and went my way, well pleased with my call.

To go back to Aranjuez. As soon as I heard that the ambassador could not put me up at Madrid, I wrote to the worthy cobbler, Don Diego, that I wanted a well-furnished room, a closet, a good bed, and an honest servant. I informed him how much I was willing to spend a month, and said I would leave Aranjuez as soon as I heard that everything was ready.

I was a good deal occupied with the question of colonising the Sierra Morena; I wrote principally on the subject of the civil government, a most important item in a scheme for a new colony. My articles pleased the Marquis Grimaldi and flattered

Mocenigo; for the latter hoped that I should become governor of the colony, and that his embassy would thereby shine with a borrowed light.

My labours did not prevent my amusing myself, and I frequented the society of those about the Court who could tell me most of the king and royal family. Don Varnier, a man of much frankness and intelligence, was my principal source of information.

I asked him one day whether the king was fond of Gregorio Squillace only because he had been once his wife's lover.

"That's an idle calumny," he replied. "If the epithet of 'chaste' can be applied to any monarch, Charles III. certainly deserves it better than any other. He has never touched any woman in his life except his wife, not only out of respect or the sanctity of marriage, but also as a good Christian. He has avoided this sin that his soul may remain pure, and so as not to have the shame of confessing it to his chaplain. He enjoys an iron constitution, sickness is unknown to him, and he is a thorough Spaniard in temperament. Ever since his marriage he has paid his duty to his wife every day, except when the state of her health compelled her to call for a truce. In such seasons this chaste husband brought down his fleshly desires by the fatigue of hunting and by abstinence. You can imagine his distress at being left a widower, for he would rather die than take a mistress. His only resource was in hunting, and in so planning out his day that he should have no time left wherein to think of women. It was a difficult matter, for he cares neither for reading nor writing, music wearies him, and conversation of a lively turn inspires him with disgust.

"He has adopted the following plan, in which he will preserve till his dying day: He dresses at seven, then goes into his closet and has his hair dressed. At eight o'clock he says his prayers, then hears mass, and when this is over he takes chocolate and an enormous pinch of snuff, over which his big nose ruminates for some minutes; this is his only pinch in the whole day. At nine o'clock he sees his ministers, and works with them till eleven. Then comes dinner, which he always takes alone, then a short visit to the Princess of the Austurias, and at twelve sharp he gets into his carriage and drives to the hunting-grounds. At seven o'clock he takes a morsel wherever he happens to be, and at eight o'clock he comes home, so tired that he often goes to sleep before he can get his clothes off. Thus he keeps down the desires of the flesh."

"Poor voluntary martyr!"

"He thought of marrying a second time, but when Adelaide of France saw his portrait she was quite frightened and refused him. He was very mortified, and renounced all thoughts of marriage; and woe to the courtier who should advise him to get a mistress!"

In further speaking of his character Don Domingo told me that the ministers had good cause for making him inaccessible, as whenever anyone did succeed in getting at him and asked a favour, he made a point of granting it, as it was at such times that he felt himself really a king.

"Then he is not a hard man, as some say?"

"Not at all. Kings seldom have the reputation they deserve. The most accessible monarchs are the least generous; they are overwhelmed with importunate requests, and their first instinct is always to refuse."

"But as Charles III. is so inaccessible he can have no opportunity of either granting or refusing."

"People catch him when he is hunting; he is usually in a good humour then. His chief defect is his obstinacy; when he has once made up his mind there is no changing it.

"He has the greatest liking for his brother, and can scarce refuse him anything, though he must be master in all things. It is thought he will give him leave to marry for the sake of his salvation; the king has the greatest horror of illegitimate children, and his brother has three already."

There were an immense number of persons at Aranjuez, who persecuted the ministers in the hope of getting employment.

"They will go back as they come," said Don Domingo, "and that is empty-handed."

"Then they ask impossibilities?"

"They don't ask anything. 'What do you want?' says a minister.

"'What your excellency will let me have.'

"'What can you do?'

"'I am ready to do whatever your excellency pleases to think best for me'

"'Please leave me. I have no time to waste.'"

That is always the way. Charles III. died a madman; the Queen of Portugal is mad; the King of England has been mad, and, as some say, is not really cured. There is nothing astonishing in it; a king who tries to do his duty is almost forced into madness by his enormous task.

I took leave of M. Mocenigo three days before he left Aranjuez, and I embraced Manucci affectionately. He had been most kind to me throughout my stay.

My cobbler had written to tell me that for the sum I had mentioned he could provide me with a Biscayan maid who could cook.. He sent me the address of my new lodging in the Calle Alcala. I arrived there in the afternoon, having started from Aranjuez in the morning.

I found that the Biscayan maid could speak French; my room was a very pleasant one, with another chamber annexed where I could lodge a friend. After I had had my effects carried up I saw my man, whose face pleased me.

I was anxious to test the skill of my cook, so I ordered her to get a good supper for me, and I gave her some money.

"I have some money," she replied, "and I will let you have the bill to-morrow."

After taking away whatever I had left with Mengs I went to Don Diego's house, and to my astonishment found it empty. I went back and asked Philippe, my man, where Don Diego was staying.

"It's some distance, sir; I will take you there tomorrow."

"Where is my landlord?"

"In the floor above; but they are very quiet people."

"I should like to see him."

"He is gone out and won't be home till ten."

At nine o'clock I was told that my supper was ready. I was very hungry, and the neatness with which the table was laid was a pleasant surprise in Spain. I was sorry that I had had no opportunity of expressing my satisfaction to Don Diego, but I sat down to supper. Then indeed I thought the cobbler a hero; the Biscayan maid might have entered into rivalry with the best cook in France. There were five dishes, including my favourite delicacy 'las criadillas', and everything was exquisite. My lodging was dear enough, but the cook made the whole arrangement a wonderful bargain.

Towards the end of supper Philippe told me that the landlord had come in, and that with my leave he would wish me a good evening.

"Shew him in by all means."

I saw Don Diego and his charming daughter enter; he had rented the house on purpose to be my landlord.

CHAPTER VI

My Amours With Donna Ignazia—Return of M. de Mocenino to Madrid

All you barons, counts, and marquises who laugh at an untitled man who calls himself a gentleman, pause and reflect, spare your disdain till you have degraded him; allow him a gentle title so long as he does gentle deeds. Respect the man that defines nobility in a new way, which you cannot understand. With him nobility is not a series of descents from father to son; he laughs at pedigrees, in which no account is taken of the impure blood introduced by wifely infidelities; he defines a nobleman as one who does noble deeds, who neither lies nor cheats, who prefers his honour to his life.

This latter part of the definition should make you tremble for your lives, if you meditate his dishonour. From imposture comes contempt, from contempt hatred, from hatred homicide, which takes out the blot of dishonour.

The cobbler Don Diego might have feared, perhaps, that I should laugh at him, when he told me he was noble; but feeling himself to be really so he had done his best to prove it to me. The fineness of his behaviour when I was in prison had given me some idea of the nobility of his soul, but he was not content with this. On the receipt of my letter, he had taken a new house only to give up the best part of it to me. No doubt he calculated on not losing in the long run, as after I had left he would probably have no difficulty in letting the apartment, but his chief motive was to oblige me.

He was not disappointed; henceforth I treated him entirely as an equal. Donna Ignazia was delighted at what her father had done for me. We talked an hour, settling our business relations over a bottle of excellent wine. I succeeded in my contention that the Biscayan cook should be kept at my expense. All the same, I wanted the girl to think that she was in Don Diego's service, so I begged him to pay her every day, as I should take all my meals at home, at all events, till the return of the ambassador. I also told him that it was a penance to me to eat alone, and begged him to keep me company at dinner and supper every day. He tried to excuse himself, and at last gave in on the condition that his daughter should take his place when he had too much work to do. As may be imagined I had anticipated this condition, and made no difficulty about it.

The next morning, feeling curious to see the way in which my landlord was lodged, I paid him a visit. I went into the little room sacred to Donna Ignazia. A bed, a chest, and a chair made up the whole furniture; but beside the bed was a desk before a picture, four feet high, representing St. Ignatius de Loyola as a fine young man, more calculated to irritate the sense than to arouse devotion.

My cobbler said to me,

"I have a much better lodging than I had before; and the rent of your room pays me for the house four times over."

"How about the furniture and the linen?"

"It will all be paid in the course of four years. I hope this house will be the dower of my daughter. It is an excellent speculation, and I have to thank you for it."

"I am glad to hear it; but what is this, you seem to be making new boots?"

"Quite so; but if you look you will see that I am working on a last which has been given me. In this way I have not to put them on, nor need I trouble myself whether they fit well or ill."

"How much do you get?"

"Thirty reals."

"That's a larger price than usual."

"Yes, but there's a great difference between my work and my leather, and the usual work and leather of the bootmakers."

"Then I will have a last made, and you shall make me a pair of shoes, if you will; but I warn you they must be of the finest skin, and the soles of morocco."

"They will cost more, and not last so long."

"I can't help that; I can't bear any but the lightest boots."

Before I left him he said his daughter should dine with me that day as he was very busy.

I called on the Count of Aranda, who received me coldly, but with great politeness. I told him how I had been treated by my parish priest and by Mengs.

"I heard about it; this was worse than your imprisonment, and I don't know what I could have done for you if you had not communicated, and obliged the priest to take out your name. Just now they are trying to annoy me with posters on the walls, but I take no notice."

"What do they want your excellency to do?"

"To allow long cloaks and low-crowned hats; you must know all about it."

"I only arrived at Madrid yesterday evening."

"Very good. Don't come here on Sunday, as my house is to be blown up."

"I should like to see that, my lord, so I will be in your hall at noon."

"I expect you will be in good company."

I duly went, and never had I seen it so full. The count was addressing the company, under the last poster threatening him with death, two very energetic lines were inscribed by the person who put up the poster, knowing that he was at the same time running his head into the noose:

Si me cogen, me horqueran,
Pero no me cogeran.

"If they catch me, they will hang me,
So I shall not let them catch me."

At dinner Donna Ignazia told me how glad she was to have me in the house, but she did not respond to all my amorous speeches after Philippe had left the room. She blushed and sighed, and then being obliged to say something, begged me to forget everything that had passed between us. I smiled, and said that I was sure she knew she was asking an impossibility. I added that even if I could forget the past I would not do so.

I knew that she was neither false nor hypocritical, and felt sure that her behaviour proceeded from devotion; but I knew this could not last long. I should have to conquer her by slow degrees. I had had to do so with other devotees who had loved me less than she, nevertheless, they had capitulated. I was therefore sure of Donna Ignazia.

After dinner she remained a quarter of an hour with me, but I refrained from any amorous attempts.

After my siesta I dressed, and went out without seeing her. In the evening when she came in for her father, who had supped with me, I treated her with the greatest politeness without shewing any ill-humour. The following day I behaved in the same manner. At dinner she told me she had broken with her lover at the beginning of Lent, and begged me not to see him if he called on me.

On Whit Sunday I called on the Count of Aranda, and Don Diego, who was exquisitely dressed, dined with me. I saw nothing of his daughter. I asked after her, and Don Diego replied, with a smile, that she had shut herself up in her room to celebrate the Feast of Pentecost. He pronounced these words in a manner and with a smile that he would not have dared to use if he had been speaking to a fellow-Spaniard. He added that she would, no doubt, come down and sup with me, as he was going to sup with his brother.

"My dear Don Diego, don't let there be any false compliments between us.
Before you go out, tell your daughter not to put herself out for me, and
that I do not pretend to put my society in comparison with that of God.
Tell her to keep her room to-night, and she can sup with me another time.
I hope you will take my message to her."

"As you will have it so, you shall be obeyed."

After my siesta, the worthy man said that Donna Ignazia thanked me and would profit by my kindness, as she did not want to see anyone on that holy day.

"I am very glad she has taken me at my word, and to-morrow I will thank her for it."

I had some difficulty in shaping my lips to this reply; for this excess of devotion displeased me, and even made me tremble for her love. I could not help laughing, however, when Don Diego said that a wise father forgives an ecstasy of love. I had not expected such a philosophic remark from the mouth of a Spaniard.

The weather was unpleasant, so I resolved to stay indoors. I told Philippe that I should not want the carriage, and that he could go out. I told my Biscayan cook that I should not sup till ten. When I was alone I wrote for some time, and in the evening the mother lit my candles, instead of the daughter, so in the end I went to bed without any supper. At nine o'clock next morning, just as I was awaking, Donna Ignazia appeared, to my great astonishment, telling me how sorry she was to hear that I had not taken any supper.

"Alone, sad, and unhappy," I replied, "I felt that abstinence was the best thing for me."

"You look downcast."

"You alone can make me look cheerful."

Here my barber came in, and she left me. I then went to mass at the
Church of the Good Success, where I saw all the handsome courtezans in
Madrid. I dined with Don Diego, and when his daughter came in with
dessert he told her that it was her fault I had gone supperless to bed.

"It shall not happen again," said she.

"Would you like to come with me to our Lady of Atocha?" said I.

"I should like it very much," she replied, with a side-glance at her father.

"My girl," said Don Diego, "true devotion and merriment go together, and the reason is that the truly devout person has trust in God and in the honesty of all men. Thus you can trust in Don Jaime as an honest man, though he has not the good fortune to be born in Spain."

I could not help laughing at this last sentence, but Don Diego was not offended. Donna Ignazia kissed her father's hands, and asked if she might bring her cousin too.

"What do you want to take the cousin for?" said Don Diego; "I will answer for Don Jaime."

"You are very kind, Don Diego, but if Ignazia likes her cousin to come I shall be delighted, provided it be the elder cousin, whom I like better than the younger."

After this arrangement the father went his way, and I sent Philippe to the stables to put in four mules.

When we were alone Ignazia asked me repentantly to forgive her.

"Entirely, if you will forgive me for loving you."

"Alas, dearest! I think I shall go mad if I keep up the battle any longer."

"There needs no battle, dearest Ignazia, either love me as I love you, or tell me to leave the house, and see you no more. I will obey you, but that will not make you happy."

"I know that. No, you shall not go from your own house. But allow me to tell you that you are mistaken in your estimate of my cousins' characters. I know what influenced you, but you do not know all. The younger is a good girl, and though she is ugly, she too has succumbed to love. But the elder, who is ten times uglier, is mad with rage at never having had a lover. She thought she had made you in love with her, and yet she speaks evil of you. She reproaches me for having yielded so easily and boasts that she would never have gratified your passion."

"Say no more, we must punish her; and the younger shall come."

"I am much obliged to you."

"Does she know that we love each other?"

"I have never told her, but she has guessed it, and pities me. She wants me to join her in a devotion to Our Lady de la Soledad, the effect of which would be a complete cure for us both."

"Then she is in love, too?"

"Yes; and she is unhappy in her love, for it is not returned. That must be a great grief."

"I pity her, and yet, with such a face, I do not know any man who would take compassion on her. The poor girl would do well to leave love alone. But as to you. . . ."

"Say nothing about me: my danger is greater than hers. I am forced to defend myself or to give in, and God knows there are some men whom it is impossible to ward off! God is my witness that in Holy Week I went to a poor girl with the smallpox, and touched her in the hope of catching it, and so losing my beauty; but God would not have it so, and my confessor blamed me, bidding me to do a penance I had never expected."

"Tell me what it is?"

"He told me that a handsome face is the index of a handsome soul, and is a gift of God, for which a woman should render thanks continually; that in attempting to destroy this beauty I had sinned, for I had endeavoured to destroy God's handiwork. After a good deal of rebuke in this style, he ordered me to put a little rouge on my cheeks whenever I felt myself looking pale. I had to submit, and I have bought a pot of rouge, but hitherto I have not felt obliged to use it. Indeed, my father might notice it, and I should not like to tell him that it is done by way of penance."

"Is your confessor a young man?"

"He is an old man of seventy."

"Do you tell him all your sins without reserve?"

"Certainly, for the smallest circumstance may be really a great sin."

"Does he ask you questions?"

"No, for he sees that I am telling him the whole truth. It is a great trial, but I have to submit to it."

"Have you had this confessor for long?"

"For two years. Before him I had a confessor who was quite unbearable. He asked me questions which made me quite indignant."

"What questions were these?"

"You must please excuse me telling you."

"Why do you go to confession so often?"

"Why? Would to God I had not good cause! but after all I only go once a week."

"That's too often."

"Not so, for when I am in mortal sin I cannot sleep at night. I am afraid of dying in my sleep."

"I pity you, dearest; I have a consolation which is denied you. I have an infinite trust in the infinite mercy of God."

The cousin arrived and we set out. We found a good many carriages in front of the church-door, and the church itself was full of devotees, both male and female. Amongst others I saw the Duchess of Villadorias, notorious for her andromania. When the 'furor uterinus' seized her, nothing could keep her back. She would rush at the man who had excited her, and he had no choice but to satisfy her passion. This had happened several times in public assemblies, and had given rise to some extraordinary scenes. I had seen her at a ball; she was still both young and pretty. As I entered the church I saw her kneeling on the stones of the church floor. She lifted her eyes, and gazed at me, as if doubtful whether she knew me or not, as she had only seen me in domino. After my devotees had prayed for half an hour, they rose to go, and the duchess rose also; and as soon as we were out of the church she asked me if I knew her. I replied in the affirmative, and she asked why I had not been to see her, and if I visited the Duchess of Benevento. I told her that I did not visit her grace, and that I should have the honour of paying her a call before long.

On our way I explained to my two companions the nature of the duchess's malady. Donna Ignazia asked me anxiously if I really meant to go and see her. She seemed reassured when I replied in the negative.

A common and to my mind a ridiculous question is which of the two sexes enjoys the generative act the more. Homer gives us Jupiter and Juno disputing on this point. Tiresias, who was once a woman, has given a correct though amusing decision on the point. A laconic answer has it that a woman enjoys the act the most because with her it is sharper, repeated more frequently, and finally because the battle is fought in her field. She is at the same time an active and passive agent, while action is indispensable to the pleasure of the man. But the most conclusive reason is that if the woman's pleasure were not the greater nature would be unjust, and she never is or can be unjust. Nothing in this universe is without its use, and no pleasure or pain is without its compensation or balance. If woman had not more pleasure than man she would not have more organs than he. The greater nervous power planted in the female organ is demonstrated by the andromania to which some women are subject, and which makes them either Messalines or martyrs. Men have nothing at all similar to this.

Nature has given to women this special enjoyment to compensate for the pains they have to undergo. What man would expose himself, for the pleasure he enjoys, to the pains of pregnancy and the dangers of childbed? But women will do so again and again; so it must be concluded that they believe the pleasure to outbalance the pain; and so it is clearly the woman who has the better share in the enjoyment. In spite of this, if I had the choice of being born again as a woman, I should say no; for in spite of my voluptuousness, a man has pleasures which a woman cannot enjoy. Though, indeed, rather than not be born again, I would be a woman, and even a brute, provided always that I had my memory, for without it I should no longer be myself.

We had some ices, and my two companions returned home with me, well pleased with the enjoyment I had given them without offending God. Donna Ignazia, who was delighted with my continence during the day, and apparently afraid of its not lasting, begged me to invite her cousin to supper. I agreed, and even did so with pleasure.

The cousin was ugly, and also a fool, but she had a great heart and was sympathetic. I knew that Donna Ignazia had told her all, and as she was no restraint on me I did not mind her being at supper, while Ignazia looked upon her as a safeguard.

The table had been laid for three, when I heard a step coming up the stairs. It was the father, and I asked him to sup with us. Don Diego was a pleasant man, as I have said, but what amused me most of all about him was his moral maxims. He knew or suspected that I was fond of his daughter, though in an honourable way; he thought my honour or his daughter's piety would be a sufficient safeguard. If he had suspected what had really happened, I do not think he would ever have allowed us to be together.

He sat beside his niece and facing his daughter, and did most of the talking, for your Spaniard, though grave, is eloquent, and fond of hearing the fine harmonies of his native tongue.

It was very hot, so I asked him to take off his waistcoat, and to tell his daughter to do just as she would if only he and his wife had been present.

Donna Ignazia had not to be entreated long before she took off her kerchief, but the poor cousin did not like having to shew us her bones and swarthy skin.

Donna Ignazia told her father how much she had enjoyed herself, and how they had seen the Duchess of Villadorias, who had asked me to come and see her.

The good man began to philosophise and to jest on her malady, and he told me some stories, germane to the question, which the girls pretended not to understand.

The good wine of La Mancha kept us at table till a late hour, and the time seemed to pass very quickly. Don Diego told his niece that she could sleep with his daughter, in the room we were in, as the bed was big enough for two. I hastened to add that if the ladies would do so I should be delighted; but Donna Ignazia blushed and said it would not do, as the room was only separated from mine by a glass door. At this I smiled at Don Diego, who proceeded to harangue his daughter in a manner which amused me extremely. He told her that I was at least twenty years older than herself, and that in suspecting me she had committed a greater sin than if she allowed me to take some slight liberty.

"I am sure," he added, "that when you go to confession next Sunday you will forget to accuse yourself of having wrongfully suspected Don Jaime of a dishonourable action."

Donna Ignazia looked at me affectionately, asked my pardon, and said she would do whatever her father liked. The cousin said nothing, and the father kissed his daughter, bade me a good night, and went away well pleased with the harangue he had delivered.

I suspected that Donna Ignazia expected me to make some attempt on her honour, and feeling sure that she would resist for the sake of appearance, I determined to leave her in peace. Next morning I got up and went into their room in the hope of playing some trick on them. However, the birds were flown, and I had no doubt that they had gone to hear mass.

Donna Ignazia came home by herself at ten o'clock. She found me alone, dressed, and writing. She told me she had been in the church for three hours.

"You have been to confession, I suppose?"

"No; I went last Sunday, and I shall wait till next Sunday."

"I am very glad that your confession will not be lengthened by any sins I have helped you to commit."

"You are wrong."

"Wrong? I understand; but you must know that I am not going to be damned for mere desires. I do not wish to torment you or to become a martyr myself. What you granted me has made me fall deeply in love with you, and it makes me shudder when I imagine that our love has become a subject of repentance with you. I have had a bad night; and it is time for me to think of my health. I must forget you, but to bring about that effect I will see you no longer. I will keep on the house, but I will not live in it. If your religion is an intelligent one, you will approve of my idea. Tell your confessor of it next Sunday, and you will see that he will approve it."

"You are right, but I cannot agree to it. You can go away if you like, and I shall say nothing, but I shall be the most unhappy girl in all Madrid."

As she spoke these words, two big tears rolled down her cheeks, and her face dropped; I was profoundly moved.

"I love you, dearest Ignazia, and I hope not to be damned for my love. I cannot see you without loving you and to this love some positive proof is essential; otherwise, I am unhappy. If I go you say you will be unhappy, and if I stay it is I that will be unhappy, my health will be ruined. But tell me which I shall do stay or go? Say."

"Stay."

"Then you must be as loving and tender as you were before."

"Alas! I promised to commit that sin no more. I tell you to stay, because I am sure that in eight or ten days we shall have become so accustomed to one another that I shall be able to love you like a father, and you will be able to take me in your arms without any amorous sentiments."

"Are you sure of this?"

"Yes, dearest, quite sure."

"You make a mistake."

"Let me be mistaken, and believe me I shall be glad to be mistaken."

"Unhappy devotee!"

"Why unhappy?"

"Nothing, nothing. I may be too long, I shall endanger . . . let us say no more about it. I will stay."

I went out more pained with her state than my own, and I felt that the best thing I could do would be to forget her, "for," said I to myself, "even if I do enjoy her once, Sunday will come again; she will confess, repent, and I shall have to begin all over again. She confessed her love, and flatters herself that she will be able to subdue it—a foolish hope, which could only exist in a mind under the dominion of prejudice."

I came home at noon, and Don Diego dined with me; his daughter did not appear till the dessert. I begged her to sit down, politely, but coldly. Her father asked her jestingly if I had paid her a visit in the night.

"I never suspected Don Jaime of such a thing," she replied, "and I only objected out of shyness."

I interrupted her by praising her modesty, and telling her that she would have done quite right to beware of me, if my sense of duty had not been stronger than any voluptuous desires inspired by her charms.

Don Diego pronounced this declaration of love as good as anything to be found in the "Morte d'Arthur."

His daughter said I was laughing at her, but Don Diego said he was certain that I was in earnest, and that I had known her before taking her to the ball.

"You are utterly mistaken," said Donna Ignazia, with some degree of fire.

"Your father is wiser than you, senora," I replied.

"What! How and when did you see me?"

"At the church where I heard mass, and you communicated, when you went out with your cousin. I followed you at some distance; you can guess the rest."

She was speechless, and her father enjoyed the consciousness of his superior intellect.

"I am going to see the bull fight," said he; "it's a fine day, and all Madrid will be there, so one must go early to get a good place. I advise you to go, as you have never seen a bull fight; ask Don Jaime to take you with him, Ignazia."

"Would you like to have my companionship?" said she, tenderly.

"Certainly I would, but you must bring your cousin, as I am in love with her."

Don Diego burst out laughing, but Ignazia said, slyly,

"It is not so impossible after all."

We went to see the splendid but barbarous spectacle in which Spaniards take so much delight. The two girls placed themselves in front of the only vacant box, and I sat behind on the second bench, which was a foot and a half higher than the first. There were already two ladies there, and much to my amusement one of them was the famous Duchess of Villadorias. She was in front of me, and sat in such a position that her head was almost between my legs. She recognized me, and said we were fortunate in meeting one another; and then noticing Donna Ignazia, who was close to her, she congratulated me in French on her charms, and asked me whether she was my mistress or my wife. I replied that she was a beauty before whom I sighed in vain. She replied, with a smile, that she was rather a sceptical person; and turning to Donna Ignazia began a pleasant and amorous discourse, thinking the girl to be as learned in the laws of love as herself. She whispered something in her ear which made Ignazia blush, and the duchess, becoming enthusiastic, told me I had chosen the handsomest girl in Madrid, and that she would be delighted to see us both at her country house.

I promised to come, as I was obliged to do, but I begged to be excused naming the day. Nevertheless, she made me promise to call on her at four o'clock the next day, telling me, much to my terror, that she would be alone. She was pretty enough, but too notorious a character; and such a visit would have given rise to talk.

Happily the fight began, and silence became general, for the Spaniards are passionately devoted of bull fighting.

So much has been written on the subject that my readers will pardon my giving a detailed account of the fight. I may say that the sport is, in my opinion, a most barbarous one, and likely to operate unfavourably on the national morals; the arena is sometimes drenched in the blood of bulls, horses, and even of the unfortunate picadores and matadores, whose sole defence is the red rag with which they irritate the bull.

When it was over I escorted the girls—who had enjoyed themselves immensely—back to the house, and made the ugly cousin stay to supper, as I foresaw that they would again sleep together.

We supped together, but it was a melancholy affair, for Don Diego was away, and I did not feel in the humour to amuse my company.

Donna Ignazia became pensive when, in reply to a question of hers, I said that it would be absolutely rude of me not to go to the duchess's.

"You will come with me some day," I added, "to dine at her country house."

"You need not look for that."

"Why not?"

"Because she is a madwoman. She talked to me in a way that would have offended me if I did not know that she fancied she was honouring me by laying aside her rank."

We rose from table, and after I had dismissed my man we sat on the balcony to wait for Don Diego and to enjoy the delicious evening breezes.

As we sat near to each other in the twilight, so favourable to lovers' vows, I looked into Donna Ignazia's eyes, and saw there that my hour had come. I clasped her to me with one arm, I clung with my lips to hers, and by the way she trembled I guessed the flame which consumed her.

"Will you go and see the duchess?"

"No, if you will promise me not to go to confession next Sunday."

"But what will he say if I do not go?"

"Nothing at all, if he understands his business. But let us talk it over a little."

We were so tightly clasped together that the cousin, like a good girl, left us, and went to the other end of the balcony, taking care to look away from us.

Without changing my position, in spite of the temptation to do so, I asked her if she felt in the humour to repent of the sin she was ready to commit.

"I was not thinking of repentance just then, but as you remind me of it,
I must tell you that I shall certainly go to confession."

"And after you have been to confession will you love me as you love me now?"

"I hope God will give me strength to offend Him no more."

"I assure you that if you continue loving me God will not give you grace, yet I feel sure that on Sunday evening you will refuse me that which you are now ready to grant."

"Indeed I will, sweetheart; but why should we talk of that now?"

"Because if I abandon myself to pleasure now I shall be more in love with you than ever, and consequently more unhappy than ever, when the day of your repentance comes. So promise me that you will not go to confession whilst I remain at Madrid, or give the fatal order now, and bid me leave you. I cannot abandon myself to love to-day knowing that it will be refused me on Sunday."

As I remonstrated thus, I clasped her affectionately in my arms, caressing her most ardently; but before coming to the decisive action I asked her again whether she would promise not to go to confession next Sunday.

"You are cruel," said she, "I cannot make you that promise for my conscience sake."

At this reply, which I had quite expected, I remained motionless, feeling sure that she must be in a state of desperate irritation at the work half begun and not concluded. I, too, suffered, for I was at the door of the sanctuary, and a slight movement would have sent me into the inmost shrine; but I knew that her torments must be greater than mine, and that she could not resist long.

Donna Ignazia was indeed in a terrible state; I had not repulsed her, but I was perfectly inactive. Modesty prevented her asking me openly to continue, but she redoubled her caresses, and placed herself in an easier position, reproaching me with my cruelty. I do not know whether I could have held out much longer, but just then the cousin turned round and told us that Don Diego was coming in.

We hastened to arrange our toilette, and to sit in a decent position. The cousin came up to us, and Don Diego, after making a few remarks, left us on the balcony, wishing us a good night. I might have begun over again, but I clung to my system of repression, and after wishing the girls good night with a melancholy air, I went to bed.

I hoped Donna Ignazia would repent and come and keep me company, but I was disappointed. They left their room early in the morning, and at noon Don Diego came to dine with me, saying his daughter had such a bad headache that she had not even gone to mass.

"We must get her to eat something."

"No, I think abstinence will do her good, and in the evening I daresay she will be able to sup with you."

I went to keep her company by her bedside after I had taken my siesta. I did my best for three hours to convince her of her folly; but she kept her eyes closed, and said nothing, only sighing when I said something very touching.

I left her to walk in St. Jerome's Park, and told her that if she did not sup with me I should understand that she did not wish to see me again. This threat had its effect. She came to table at supper-time, but she looked pale and exhausted. She ate little, and said nothing, for she knew not what to say. I saw that she was suffering, and I pitied her from my heart.

Before going to bed she asked me if I had been to see the duchess. She seemed somewhat cheered when I answered in the negative. I told her that she might satisfy herself of the truth of my reply by asking Philippe, who had taken my note begging her grace to excuse me for that day.

"But will you go another day?"

"No, dearest, because I see it would grieve you."

She gave a sigh of content, and I embraced her gently, and she left me as sad as I was.

I could see that what I asked of her was a great deal; but I had good grounds for hope, as I knew her ardent disposition. It was not God and I that were disputing for her, but her confessor and I. If she had not been a Catholic I should have won her the first day.

She had told me that she would get into trouble with her confessor if she did not go to him as usual; she had too much of fine Spanish honour in her to tell him what was not true, or to endeavour to combine her love with her religion.

The Friday and the Saturday passed without any events of consequence. Her father, who could not blind himself to our love any longer, trusted, I suppose, to his daughter's virtue, and made her dine and sup with me every day. On Saturday evening Donna Ignazia left me sadder than ever, and turned her head away when I would have kissed her as usual. I saw what was the matter; she was going to communicate the next day. I admired her consistency, in spite of myself, and pitied her heartily; for I could guess the storm that must be raging in her breast. I began to repent having demanded all, and wished I had been contented with a little.

I wished to be satisfied with my own eyes, and got up early on Sunday morning and followed her. I knew that she would call for her cousin, so I went on to the church. I placed myself by the sacristy-door, where I could see without being seen.

I waited a quarter of an hour, then they came in, and after kneeling down for a few moments, separated, each going to her own confessor.

I only noticed Donna Ignazia; I saw her going to the confessional, and the confessor turning towards her.

I waited patiently. I thought the confession would never come to an end. "What is he saying?" I repeated to myself as I saw the confessor speaking to her now and again.

I could bear it no longer, and I was on the point of going away when I saw her rise from her knees.

Donna Ignazia, looking like a saint, came to kneel in the church, but out of my sight. I thought she would come forward to receive the Holy Communion at the end of the Mass that was being said, but instead of that she went towards the door, rejoined her cousin and they left the church. I was astonished. My heart was seized with a pang of remorse.

"It's all over," I said to myself. "The poor girl has made a sincere and full confession, she has avowed her love, and the priest's cruel duty has made him refuse her absolution.

"All is lost. What will come of it?"

"My peace of mind and hers require me to leave her.

"Wretch that I am, to have lost all for all! I should have made allowance for the peculiar Spanish character.

"I might have enjoyed her by surprise now and again; the difficulty would have added piquancy to the intrigue. I have behaved as if I were once more twenty, and I have lost all.

"At dinner she will be all sad and tearful. I must find some way out of this terrible situation."

Thus soliloquising, I came home ill pleased with the line of conduct I had adopted.

My hairdresser was waiting for me, but I sent him away, and told my cook not to serve my dinner till I ordered it; then, feeling the need of rest, I flung myself on my bed and slept profoundly till one o'clock.

I got up and ordered dinner to be brought in, and sent a message to the father and daughter that I was expecting them.

My surprise may be imagined when Donna Ignazia appeared in a costume of black velvet, adorned with ribbons and lace. In my opinion there is no more seductive costume in Europe when the wearer is pretty.

I also noticed that every feature of her face breathed peace and calm; I had never seen her looking so well, and I could not help congratulating her. She replied with a smile, and I gave her a kiss, which she took as meekly as a lamb.

Philippe arrived, and we sat down to table. I saw that my fair sweetheart had crossed the Rubicon; the day was won.

"I am going to be happy," said she, "but let us say nothing, and it will come of itself."

However, I did not conceal my bliss, and made love to her whenever the servant was out of the room. She was not only submissive, but even ardent.

Before we left the table she asked me if I still loved her.

"More than ever, darling; I adore you."

"Then take me to the bull fight."

"Quick! Fetch the hairdresser."

When my hair was done I made an elaborate toilette, and burning with impatience we set out on foot, as I was afraid we should not secure a good place if we waited till the carriage was ready. We found a fine box with only two persons in it, and Ignazia, after glancing round, said she was glad that the detestable duchess was not anywhere near us.

After some fine sport my mistress begged me to take her to the Prado, where all the best people in Madrid are to be seen.

Donna Ignazia leant on my arm, seemed proud to be thought mine, and filled me with delight.

All at once we met the Venetian ambassador and his favourite, Manucci. They had just arrived from Aranjuez. We greeted each other with due Spanish politeness, and the ambassador paid me a high compliment on the beauty of my companion. Donna Ignazia pretended not to understand, but she pressed my arm with Spanish delicacy.

After walking a short distance with us M. de Mocenigo said he hoped I would dine with him on the following day, and after I had nodded acquiescence in the French style we parted.

Towards the evening we took some ices and returned home, and the gentle pressure of my arm on the way prepared me for the bliss I was to enjoy.

We found Don Diego on the balcony waiting for us. He congratulated his daughter on her pleasant appearance and the pleasure she must have taken in my society.

Charmed with papa's good humour, I asked him to sup with us, and he accepted, and amused us with his witty conversation and a multitude of little tales that pleased me exceedingly. He made the following speech on leaving us, which I give word for word, but I cannot give the reader any idea of the inimitable Spanish gravity with which it was delivered.

"Amigo Senior Don Jaime, I leave you here to enjoy the cool air with my daughter. I am delighted at your loving her, and you may be assured that I shall place no obstacle in the way of your becoming my son-in-law as soon as you can shew your titles of nobility."

When he was gone, I said to his daughter,—

"I should be only too happy, if it could be managed; but you must know that in my country they only are called nobles who have an hereditary right to rule the state. If I had been born in Spain I should be noble, but as it is I adore you, and I hope you will make me happy."

"Yes, dearest, but we must be happy together; I cannot suffer any infidelity."

"I give you my word of honour that I will be wholly faithful to you."

"Come then, 'corazon mio', let us go in."

"No, let us put out the lights, and stay here a quarter of an hour. Tell me, my angel, whence comes this unexpected happiness?"

"You owe it to a piece of tyranny which drove me to desperation. God is good, and I am sure He would not have me become my own executioner. When I told my confessor that I could not help loving you, but that I could restrain myself from all excess of love, he replied that this self-confidence was misplaced, as I had already fallen. He wanted me to promise never to be alone with you again, and on my refusing to do so he would not give me absolution.

"I have never had such a piece of shame cast on me, but I laid it all in the hands of God, and said, 'Thy will be done.'

"Whilst I heard mass my mind was made up, and as long as you love me I shall be yours, and yours only. When you leave Spain and abandon me to despair, I shall find another confessor. My conscience holds me guiltless; this is my comfort. My cousin, whom I have told all, is astonished, but then she is not very clever."

After this declaration, which put me quite at my ease, and would have relieved me of any scruples if I had had them, I took her to my bed. In the morning, she left me tired out, but more in love with her than ever.

The End